A Recent History of Lesbian and Gay Psychology

D1564522

This ground-breaking text explores the contemporary history of how psychological research, practice, and theory have engaged with gay and lesbian movements in the United States and beyond over the last 50 years. Peter Hegarty examines the main strands of research in lesbian and gay psychology that have emerged since the de-pathologizing of homosexuality in the 1970s that followed from the recognition of homophobia and societal prejudice.

The author details the expansion of 'lesbian and gay psychology' to 'LGB' to 'LGBT psychology' via its paradigm shifts, legal activism, and shifts in policy makers' and mental health professionals' goals in regard to sexual and gender minorities. For the first time, the origins of the concepts, debates, and major research programs that have made up the field of LGBT psychology have been drawn together in a single historical narrative, making this a unique resource. A case is made that psychology has only very lately come to consider the needs and issues of transgender and intersex people and that LGB paradigms need to be critically interrogated to understand how they can be best brokered to bring about social change for such groups.

A Recent History of Lesbian and Gay Psychology will serve as an advanced historical introduction to this field's recent history and current concerns, and will inform both those who have been a part of this history and students who are new to the field.

Peter Hegarty teaches social psychology and the history of psychology at the University of Surrey where he also leads on research impact and public engagement for psychology. He has published extensively on the social psychology and history of sexuality and gender in psychology. This is his second book.

A Recent History of Lesbian and Gay Psychology

From Homophobia to LGBT

Peter Hegarty

Routledge
Taylor & Francis Group

LONDON AND NEW YORK

First published 2018
by Routledge
2 Park Square, Milton Park, Abingdon, Oxon OX14 4RN

and by Routledge
711 Third Avenue, New York, NY 10017

Routledge is an imprint of the Taylor & Francis Group, an informa business

British Library Cataloguing in Publication Data
A catalogue record for this book is available from the British Library

Library of Congress Cataloging in Publication Data
A catalog record for this book has been requested

ISBN: 978-1-138-67939-9 (hbk)
ISBN: 978-1-138-67940-5 (pbk)
ISBN: 978-1-315-56344-2 (ebk)

Typeset in Baskerville
by Taylor & Francis Books

Contents

Preface

The writing of this book has a longer past than its history. It's my attempt to capture something of teaching mostly undergraduate courses on this topic at Stanford (1997–1999), Yale (2001–2002), Michigan (2006), and Surrey (2008–2012), and at the University of Michigan's International LGBT Psychology Summer Institutes, 2008 and 2010. As I moved around, so too did this field. At Stanford, this course was called 'Lesbian and Gay Perspectives on Psychology.' By the time it was taught at Surrey it had become 'LGBT Psychology.' I always aimed these courses to raise questions beyond the specifics of LGBT people's lives and experience, and to reach for broader relevance for psychology. Indeed in 2013 and 2014 Surrey students encountered many of the ideas here in a course titled 'General Psychology.' This book similarly insists that LGBT psychology is of *general* relevance to psychologists and their historians.

In the past 20 years, I have learned a lot from listening to what sense students make of ideas, writings, and findings in this field. I always allowed students to write their research papers about any topic, and their choices taught me how history moves fast. Even at Stanford between 1997 and 1999 students wrote far fewer essays focused on HIV/AIDS and more essays about transgender. Progressive change has not always been guaranteed. In 2006, many Michigan students took up the task of refuting psychiatrist Robert Spitzer's study on conversion therapies, an essay topic that would have seemed uninteresting and even backward to students in the late 1990s. At Surrey, I felt no need to teach about biological models of sexuality at all, as they were neither of particular interest to the UK students, nor relevant to their socio-political context. Nonetheless, students have *always* chosen to write about prejudice, always about lesbian mothers, and always about under-researched intersecting identities. I have taken the same freedom here to write about what I know and what interests me most in this history. Consequently, this book also draws together ideas that I have expressed as a social psychologist, critical psychologist, and historian of psychology. This emphasis is clearest in Chapters 5 and 6 where I place some research that I did myself in the larger context of the field.

I mean this book to be of use to students who are similarly interested in developing their own perspective on LGBT psychology. Those who aim to do so can be bothered by naysayers inside and outside the head who insist that this area is marginal, trivial, unscientific, or biased by political correctness. Many students are not given a chance to consider this area of psychology as a specialty at all. Others continue to be told – as I was – that specializing in this area might be well-intentioned, but that ultimately and inevitably it is ill-informed and career-limiting. (Especially now!) Moreover, when working in LGBT psychology projects, I have been *most* demanded to think critically, holistically, reflexively, and practically, and these tensions demand the best psychology from psychologists. Specializing in this area has not limited my career, quite the opposite.

In writing that last sentence, I am haunted by the knowledge that acknowledging that LGBT psychologists can succeed immediately invokes in some people the response that then, surely, the field's major fights are in the past, and so that the field is pointless (and that those that would think otherwise are asking for special favors). One of my motivations to write about this field *historically* is to get past the schema in which the field's past achievements seem inevitable, trivial, or to-be-assumed, whilst those in the future seem so unlikely or unimportant that it would be unwise to pursue them. Indeed, I take the many ways in which people 'come out' as just about anything, use the suffix *-phobia* to call attention to an under-recognized prejudice, and seek to add letters beyond the LGBT taxonomy in psychology all to recognize that 'lesbian and gay psychology' achieved something of generalizable usefulness, whose importance went beyond the lesbians and gay men to whom it initially applied.

I also hope this book will interest scholars looking for a single source on the recent history of lesbian and gay-affirmative psychology. This book covers events during the period roughly from the early 1970s to the end of the 2000s. Psychological research – not psychotherapy, psychiatry, health psychology, or lesbian, gay, or queer studies – is at its center. I originally planned to take the book all the way up to the present, but in writing it over 2015–2016 'the present' changed – again – with such rapidity that it first seemed difficult, and only later *unwise*, to do so. At the start of the year, the *Obergefell* judgment appeared to suggest to some that the LGBT movement had done its job and could wrap up and go home. I am completing it as President-elect Trump is assembling a team unambiguous in their intent to undo the history that is described here. This book shows how lesbian and gay psychology was formed in response to external events, through which we continue to live.

When I first taught this course in the late 1990s, I was very enamored of the possibilities opened up by translating lesbian, gay, and queer theory into psychology. In writing this book I also became more and more appreciative of the work carried out in the 1970s and 1980s, which created the conditions under which such translations could be *understood* within psychology. And so, if you or anyone else is questioning why you would ever be so naïve as to think that you and your friends could do something useful in LGBT psychology, then I hope this book will provide the backchatty answer that small groups of people, with sustained effort, can create meaningful change over medium chunks of historical time. Indeed, after reading this book, you might want to reply to the naysayers – name me a kind of psychology that has achieved more in recent history against such odds.

1 Normative creativity

In 1988 the feminist therapist Laura Brown delivered an address as president of the 'Division for Lesbian and Gay Concerns,' Division 44 of the American Psychological Association. Brown called for a psychology that would go beyond the discipline's existing heterosexist knowledge base by making the experiences of lesbians and gay men central. Drawing on feminist thinking, she urged continual questioning of psychology's positivist epistemology 'which assumes that phenomena are either A or B,' and an utter rejection of definitions of reality that either entirely ignore lesbian and gay men's experiences, or marginalize them as peripheral 'special topics.' The costs of such erasure and marginalization were very high, because the experiences of lesbians and gay men – and other marginalized groups – had *transformative* potential. In Brown's view, such lives, shaped by their experiences of biculturalism and marginality, required the development of 'normative creativity'; a 'terrifying and exhilarating' process of making up norms of how to be, live, and love, when the dominant culture provided none at all, or provided only norms that worked against one's very being.[1]

Feminist therapy was a pivotal space in the late 1980s in which lesbian-affirmative perspectives in psychology took shape.[2] Brown located her speech in the recent historical context, emphasizing particularly the de-pathologization of homosexuality by the American Psychiatric Association and American Psychological Association in the early 1970s. But she knew that history had moved on since then. Defining the epistemology of this hoped-for future lesbian/gay paradigm of psychology in liminal spaces between constructed binaries, Brown embraced multiple rather than singular truths. A lesbian/gay psychology might not only be productive in individual lives, but might further transform all of psychology through 'a dialectical tension' that would stimulate new forms of inquiry. In the 1990s, calls for such dialectical transformation in knowledge from minority experience, such as Brown's, became institutionalized as 'social constructionist' or 'critical' perspectives in some quarters *and* called out as the worst excesses of 'political correctness' in others. Psychology would not need to wait until Brown's vision was fulfilled before it became a field that included multiple contradictory claims on truth and value.

From the advantaged perspective of the present it is possible to look back cynically at the shortcomings of Brown's early vision, and the forms of lesbian and gay psychology that followed. The Division of the APA to which Brown spoke is now called the 'Society for the Psychological Study of Lesbian, Gay, Bisexual and Transgender Issues.' Although much of Brown's argument rests on the affordances of transcendence that live at the margins and liminal in-between spaces of the binary gender system, both bi- and trans- people and their experiences and knowledges went unmentioned in her vision. Moreover, in formulating a lesbian/gay vision, Brown overlooked HIV/AIDS entirely, the most pressing issue for gay and bisexual men in the late 1980s, and one that was already prompting a paradigm shift among a wide range of psychologists. Whilst these particularities matter, a presentist criticism of the gaps in Brown's vision would not do justice to her own understanding of the dangers of unkind historical hindsight. Brown recognized the value of ambivalence and multiplicity in historical thinking at moments when paradigms shift, and reminded her listeners that a new paradigm 'in no way denigrates that which has been done before and will continue to be done by way of research and practice in the field.'[3]

Brown was not alone in noticing that lesbian and gay psychology had developed to the point where its assumptions could be productively challenged. In 1987, British psychologist Celia Kitzinger proposed a radical feminist alternative to 'lesbian-affirmative' psychology which assumed that 'patriarchy (not capitalism or sex roles or socialization or individual sexist men) is the root of all forms of oppression; that all men benefit from it and maintain it and are, therefore, our political enemies.'[4] Kitzinger's work was deeply informed by social studies of science and she critiqued the *rhetoric* by which lesbian and gay psychology justified itself, such as the rhetoric of empirical science and its claim to represent authentic 'experience.' Central to her critique was the charge that lesbian and gay psychology was complicit with an ideology of liberal humanism that promised individual adjustment to patriarchal society, such that psychology effectively distracted people from more substantive structural changes. For Kitzinger, lesbian and gay-affirmative psychology was already bringing about a different future – and going in entirely wrong directions.[5] If Brown imagined that lesbians might transform psychology, Kitzinger hoped they would abandon it.

These two critical perspectives are part of a longer tradition of critical and conceptual engagement with what became 'LGBT psychology' by those who care about the empowerment of LGBT people, and this book is written in that spirit. The *recent history* of this field has rarely been drawn together. More commonly, history has been told in terms of a break between the (bad) past and the (better) present in the early 1970s when homosexuality became de-pathologized. Brown singled out the de-pathologization of homosexuality as *the* historical event which shaped the context of her speaking most obviously. Kitzinger repeatedly ventured, to rhetorical effect, that lesbians were much better off being labeled as sick than as being adjusted by affirmative psychologists. Histories that focus on the century before the 1970s describe the emergence of sexology in the late nineteenth century, the era to which the French philosopher Michel Foucault famously dated the introduction of the idea that the homosexual was a distinct kind of person.[6] Histories chart how the psychoanalytic movement, the development of hormonal interventions and the rise of the sex survey all contributed to making sexuality 'psychological.'[7]

One study looms particularly large in historical accounts of lesbian and gay *psychology*. In the 1950s, psychologist Evelyn Hooker administered several projective tests – such as the Rorschach inkblot test – to matched pairs of gay and straight men. Whilst the straight men were difficult to recruit, the Mattachine Society, a homophile group, collaborated with Hooker to recruit gay research subjects. Experts in interpreting such tests rated each man for 'adjustment,' and attempted to guess his sexuality from his test results alone. Importantly, even such respected experts in Rorschach interpretation as Hooker's friend Bruno Klopfer could not tell who was who better than guessing at chance.[8] Hooker's experiment has become a foundational 'origin story' for lesbian and gay psychologists, an explanation of how 'we' in the field became who we are. It is also understood as initiating an empirical tradition of defeating social prejudice with the kinds of facts that psychologists and our science can produce.

Whilst Hooker's work certainly was intended and executed to produce progressive knowledge, accounts can forget Hooker's normative creativity when it is remembered simply as demonstrating 'no difference' between gay and straight men. There were *two* kinds of research participants in Hooker's experiment: the gay and straight men, and the experts who attempted to distinguish them. Hooker's work was part of a larger historical trajectory by which the Rorschach test reversed its gaze away from peering into the personalities of homosexuals and began to reflect on the stereotypes and assumptions of psychiatrists who assumed that a distinct 'homosexual personality' existed, which they hoped the test could detect.[9] The rhetorical power of her study depended upon reversing the empirical gaze up the power hierarchy. Arguably the most important research subject in the study was not any gay man, but the Rorschach expert Bruno Klopfer. Let's be clear, such an experiment does not add up to either Brown's paradigm shift or Kitzinger's radical rejection of liberal humanism. Nonetheless, this kind of reversal recurs often because lesbian and gay psychologists must do more than assert empirical similarities and differences to achieve progressive change. Hooker's experiment tells a different story about who 'we' are if it is remembered that it was a use of the scientific method *and* a critique of a set of scientific claims that served to justify the oppression of gay men and lesbians by making us into objects of interminable suspicion and fear.

Brown's call for a new paradigm also expressed her intuition that it is *norms* that undo lesbians and gay men, and that it is norms that lesbians and gay men need to recreate in their own lives. Her call occurs at the same time that scholars in lesbian, gay, and queer studies, an interdisciplinary study that was gaining recognition in the late 1980s, drew attention to the dynamics of *heteronormativity*; the ideology that privileges heterosexuality as the ontological ground for everything (including 'society' and 'nature'). How does normativity work, and how to you creatively respond to it? In an earlier book, I distinguished two types of normativity that locate difference in exceptional people.[10] Drawing on the history of the statistics, I called these two *Queteletian* and *Galtonian* normativity. Queteletian normativity assumes that unusual people are tragically ill-fated, and worries about how they might threaten society. If parents can visualize no bright future for their child who comes out or expresses a wish to dress, play, or identify in a way that is not 'normal' for their assigned gender, or assume that an array of others will harm their child whenever this difference is noticed, then those parents are caught up in Queteletian normativity. Galtonian normativity emerged later and is a kind of creative response to Queteletian normativity that is less about preserving the status quo than configuring optimism. Galtonian normativity is optimistic about what unusual people may become; think of the place that gifted children occupy in eugenic fantasies, for example. Galtonian normativity doesn't demand that exceptional people become more normal; it obliges them to bring about the future that they are imagined to promise. If employers believe that LGB people's experience of marginalization or unique combinations of gender traits diversify leadership or bring creativity to a project and might give business a competitive edge then they are engaging in Galtonian normativity.[11] In imagining normative creativity, Laura Brown was putting this kind of demand on our shoulders.

In *Gentlemen's Disagreement*, I considered how discourses about exceptionally intelligent children and adults (who were largely gendered male) shifted between the logics of Galtonian and Queteletian normativity, particularly when high intelligence signaled queerness. Whilst the events in that book ended in the mid-1950s, I argued there that this understanding of normativity has relevance for the present. Hence, I am not surprised that when Brown refused to rest with the simple defense of lesbians and gay men from Queteletian normativity, she drew on a notion about the intellect – creativity. In *Gentlemen's Disagreement*, I examined what went wrong when Lewis Terman entrusted in particular gifted children what he called 'the promise of youth,' particularly when they grew up queer. Galtonian normativity can create binding obligations that overlook how structural conditions and marginalization limit the capacity of the exceptional to bring about the change that their difference appears to others to promise. Lesbian and gay psychologists have often had to creatively transform psychology to achieve progress. Obliging queer people to meet unrealistic and romantic ideals to transform psychology, corporations, or anything else through acts of genius is asking a lot. Galtonian normativity requires us to see that hope and optimism have a darker side.

This book is organized into five further chapters. Chapter 2 describes the emergence of affirmative approaches to lesbians and gay men in the 1970s and 1980s. Critical to this chapter is my claim that 'affirmation of lesbians and gay men' left the helping professions in a state that Eve Sedgwick has called 'open season on gay kids.'[12] Whilst psychiatric pathologization was the most obvious 'other' that lesbian and gay psychology defined itself against, the continuing pathologization of children who seemed most likely to grow up lesbian, gay, bisexual, or trans constitutes a foundational dilemma and limit to the field. Chapter 3 examines how government inaction in response to HIV/AIDS prompted new forms of science that appeared to offer great promise to psychology in the 1980s, and which contributed to the broadening out of gay-affirmative perspectives in psychology. I consider how lesbian and gay psychology formulated its objects around *prejudice*, including its causes and consequences, and wrestled with the conflicts in values created by a commitment to affirmation on the one hand and a value-neutral empiricist discourse on the other.

Nowhere did lesbian and gay psychologists challenge heteronormative society more persistently and effectively than in the courts, and Chapter 4 considers legal activism by the American Psychological Association from the 1980s into recent support for equal marriage. Lesbian and gay psychological research aligned with legal strategy in ways that are distinct to the USA, were organized around the concept of prejudice, and differentiated psychology from other disciplines that took 'sexuality' as an object of knowledge in this decade. In Chapter 5, I review social psychological evidence that refutes the claim that biological models of sexuality constitute a kind of 'strategic essentialism' which played a role in ameliorating heterosexist prejudice. As the shortcomings of such biological theories became evident in the late 1990s, theories of flexible sexualities that emphasized gender differences rather than gender similarities introduced new definitions of sexuality, suggesting that not only psychology, but the very experience of sexuality was itself in a state of historical flux.

In Chapter 6, I examine the American Psychological Association's 2009 Report on Transgender Issues.[13] This report provides an early and developed exemplar of how marginalized identity groups claim recognition in ways that cite the recent history of lesbian and gay psychology. The shift in recognition in the APA from LG to LGB to LGBT over the last 30 years asks lesbian and gay psychology to be a paradigm for how social movements and psychology can creatively come together, to make good on the promises of Galtonian normativity. I examine what the report says about this history, and what gets lost and what gets promised in making 'LGB psychology' the historical basis for transgender psychology, in both realist and analogical terms.

Notes

1 Brown (1989, p. 452).
2 See the work published in *Women and Therapy* in this period, particularly Rothblum (1988).
3 Brown (1989, p. 455).
4 Kitzinger (1987, p. 64).
5 See Brown (1992); Kitzinger & Perkins (1993).
6 Foucault (1978).
7 See Minton (2002), Terry (1999), Rosario (1997).
8 Hooker (1957, 1958, 1993).
9 Hegarty (2003).
10 Hegarty (2013).
11 See e.g., Snyder (2006).
12 Sedgwick (1991).
13 American Psychological Association (2009).

2   Revolutionary science

Laura Brown ventured that change in lesbian and gay psychology happened according to the model of 'paradigm shifts' described by philosopher Thomas Kuhn.[1] For Kuhn, a paradigm was, first and foremost, a model problem that organized both scientists' formal knowledge and tacit understanding of what a science is about and the kinds of questions it should address. Kuhn critiqued the assumption that knowledge develops by accumulation, and instead foregrounded moments of revolutionary change in science – *paradigm shifts* – periods when it becomes unclear which of several paradigms should have epistemological priority in making the best sense of reality. When paradigms change, not only do new questions open up, but old ones close down, cease to be asked, and fall out of interest in the science. In this chapter, I examine the contours and limits of the paradigm shift away from a disease paradigm to a stigma paradigm for making sense of homosexuality that led up to Brown's speech.

The revolution of the non-patient

In the late 1960s, it was far from agreed among early gay liberationist thinkers that alliances with mental health professions would be possible or desirable in the future at all. Writing in *The Ladder*, the publication of the Daughters of Bilitis, Frank Kameny, who led the Washington DC branch of the Mattachine Society, argued that *no* homophile organization had successfully engaged with research, or needed to try. Kameny had for years conceptualized the diagnosis of homosexuality as one of his targets, and considered research about the origins of homosexuality to be 'symptomatic of a thinly-veiled defensive feeling of inferiority, of uncertainty, of inequality, of insecurity – and most important, of lack of comfortable self-acceptance.' Describing Evelyn Hooker's work as a rare exception, and as a 'bulwark' against psychiatric propaganda, but one that is 'not needed, in strict logic,' Kameny anticipated in the mid-1960s Brown's later concern that lesbian and gay politics do more than assert the case against group differences. Strictly speaking, the health, normalcy or rights of homosexuals should not be held hostage to finding such results.[2]

Kameny's suspicions about the psychologists of his day were right. In 1967, Hooker chaired a Task Force of the National Institute of Mental Health (NIMH) on homosexuality which included psychiatrists, psychologists, sexologists, and sociologists among its members.[3] The Task Force Report mapped out possible 'scientific' projects around homosexuality and was completed in October 1969, only months after the Stonewall riots in New York City, a moment that more than any other brought awareness and energy to the gay liberation movement. Hooker failed to achieve a full consensus within her Task Force. In particular the Report's opposition to state sodomy laws, which criminalized homosexual acts, was critiqued as mere political opinion rather than scientific analysis by some. The Report was deemed controversial and its publication was delayed. It was first published in 1970 by the homophile publication *ONE*.[4] The NIMH published it later in 1972, by which time gay activists had begun to apply far more direct methods to change hearts and minds in psychiatry.

Led by Kameny, lesbian and gay activists began to apply techniques such as *direct action* that they learned from the civil rights movement to the medical establishment, protesting the meeting of the American Medical Association in San Francisco in 1968, and the meetings of the American Psychiatric Association from 1970 onward. Following discussion between sympathetic psychiatrists and pro-testers, members of gay and lesbian liberation movement Frank Kameny, Larry Littlejohn, Del Martin, Lille Vincenz, and Jack Baker organized a panel on 'Lifestyles of Non-Patient Homosexuals.' The language mirrored Hooker's own language. She had also described her study as one of 'non-patient homosexuals.' The diagnostic model was so hegemonic that homosexuals who were *not* patients were the unusual marked category. The panellists spoke from experience and rejected psychiatric expertise directly and forcefully. Demonstrators also continued to speak from experience in other ways. By the end of the 1971 convention Kameny had voiced demands for the deletion of homosexuality from the Associa-tion's *Diagnostic and Statistical Manual* (*DSM*) of psychiatric disorders, where it had been included since the first edition in 1952.

The constitution of the panel on homosexuality at the 1972 meeting made strikingly visible the incompatibility between speaking about homosexuality from experience and speaking with psychiatric authority. The panellists included two liberal psychiatrists, Judd Marmor and Robert Seidenberg; two activists, Frank Kameny and Barbara Gittings; and one 'Dr Anonymous,' a hooded psychiatrist who spoke through a microphone that disguised his voice, and who spoke about and for closeted psychiatrists. After the 1973 meeting, the psychiatrist Robert Spitzer arranged a panel discussion with the Association's Committee on Nomenclature which included only psychiatrists: Irvine Bibber and Charles Socarides, who favored retaining the diagnosis, and Judd Marmor and Richard Green, who favored abandoning it. The Board of Trustees subsequently voted to delete homosexuality in 1973. However, a group led by Bieber and Socarides called for a referendum of APA members to vote on the question. The question of whether gay men and lesbians would be deemed categorically sick now hung on the views of the majority of American psychiatrists.[5]

What might have been expected of this vote? In the early 1970s, several surveys – sometimes carried out by lesbian and gay activists – suggested that mental health professionals were far from being uniformly negative in their views about homosexuality. Many psychiatrists and psychologists agreed with Hooker's Task Force in opposing sodomy laws, and many were willing to pursue clients' goals of self-acceptance rather than imposing sexual orientation change as the goal of intervention.[6] Lesbian and gay activists were particularly angered by the behavioral intervention of administering electric shocks to punish or extinguish arousal in response to homoerotic stimuli. Ethical controversies surrounded coercive behavior treatments such as these in the early 1970s, as these treatments resembled the dynamics of Stanley Milgram's famous experiment in which many people were willing to administer painful and harmful electric shocks to a stranger in a learning experiment.[7] One survey found that many behavior therapists socialized with gay people personally and believed that homosexuality was not an illness. Nonetheless, the same behavior therapists still believed that they had successfully 'cured' homosexual patients.[8] As in Milgram's experiment, psychologists and psychiatrists were influenced by situational norms that outweighed their private attitudes in determining their actions towards others, including administering painful electric shocks to them. In the one survey that truly mattered, the members of the American Psychiatric Association voted by a majority of 58% to 37% to repeal the diagnosis. However, to satisfy dissenters, the Association named 'sexual orientation disturbance' to allow the continued treatment of homosexuals who *wanted* to be treated. The de-pathologization of homosexuality was far from over in 1974. The International Classification of Diseases of the World Health Organization listed homosexuality as a mental illness from ICD-9 in 1977 until ICD-10 in 1990.

New paradigms, new problems

Beyond these concrete battles with the psychiatric establishment, gay liberationists argued forcefully and repeatedly that it was not the homosexual, but oppressive society, that was sick. The concept of 'homophobia' circulated in the gay liberationist movement in New York City, appeared in a *New York Times* article about gay liberation in 1969, and was later popularized by the heterosexual psychologist George Weinberg in his short book *Society and the Healthy Homosexual*. 'Homophobia' was a conceptual tool that deflected the normalization that psychiatry brought to homosexuality back onto society in general. The first sentence of Weinberg's book made this deflection literal: 'I would never consider a patient healthy unless he had overcome his prejudice against homosexuality.'[9] When *psychologists* begin to conceptualize prejudices toward a particular social group, it is often a sign that attitudes in society and in the profession are changing, and that prejudice itself is on the wane.[10] Empirical studies of *prejudice* against homosexuality date from the early 1970s also. The earliest was published in 1971 in the marginal journal *Psychological Reports*, and in the years to 1974, thirteen psychological studies on homophobia were published, including the first study examining educational interventions to reduce it.[11]

Gay men and lesbians were far from being the only, or indeed the most prominent, minority group contesting and changing the way that they were represented by mental health professions in the early 1970s. Movements for liberation along lines of gender, race, sexuality, age, and class often intersected and only later did the terms 'gay' and 'lesbian' take on their current meanings as references to discrete groups of people defined by sexual identity. 'Lesbian and gay' was not an inevitable grouping. Many lesbians viewed their oppression in terms of gender rather than sexuality, and left gay liberationist groups because of the sexism of their gay male collaborators.[12] Poet and author Adrienne Rich critiqued psychoanalytic theories, including new feminist theories, that left unexplained the question of why women might ever become heterosexual in the first place. She detailed the very wide range of physical, affective, economic, and intellectual mechanisms that rewarded or compelled heterosexuality among women, often by obfuscating the knowledge that women throughout history had often chosen alternatives to heterosexuality, and described a lesbian continuum that stepped beyond such social constraints.[13] Monique Wittig went one ontological step further, describing the category of 'woman' as created within heterosexuality's contract, such that lesbians, who had escaped it, were no longer bound to the category of 'women' at all.[14] The Association for Women in Psychology also protested psychology's exclusion of and representation of women, and became a point from which many lesbian psychologists in the American Psychological Association organized their politics in the 1970s.[15]

Within psychology, lesbian and gay voices emerged within structures put in place in response to protests representing the interests of Black and women psychologists. Following a public challenge to George Miller's 1969 presidential address at the American Psychological Association meeting by several Black psychologists, the APA instituted the Board of Social and Ethical Responsibility for Psychology (BSERP). BSERP had an uneasy time in making psychology more accountable on controversial social issues concerning social inequalities in the 1970s and 1980s, and it was retired and superseded by the Board for the Advancement of Psychology in the Public Interest in 1990.[16] New social movements' claims for representation and recognition quickly found a place in APA Division 17 for Counseling Psychology, which included a section devoted to women's concerns from 1970 onward and which led work conceptualizing the competencies required to work with racially and ethnically diverse clients by the decade's end.[17]

The repeal of the diagnosis in the American Psychiatric Association was but one of several moves within professional societies towards more affirmative positions in the early 1970s. Although less often remembered, gay liberationists engaged psychology as well as psychiatry in this period with activist tactics. The newly formed Association for Gay Psychologists (AGP), a mostly male group organized in 1973 in California, 'zapped' the screening of a film on behavior therapy to 'cure' homosexuality at the 1973 meeting of the American Psychological Association.[18] From 1974 onward, a Task Force on the Status of Lesbian and Gay Male Psychologists reported to BSERP. One of their first actions was to propose the following resolution agreed by the Council of Representatives of the APA at their 1974 meeting:

Homosexuality per se implies no impairment in judgment, stability, reliability, or general social or vocational capacities;

Furthermore, the American Psychological Association urges all mental health professionals to take the lead in removing the stigma of mental illness that has long been associated with homosexual orientations.[19]

This resolution was the first of several that the APA would make in support of lesbian, gay, bisexual, and transgender concerns in the decades to come.[20] The resolution crystalized the rationale for the then-new lesbian and gay psychology, and deserves sustained attention for that reason. Notice that first of all, *similarities* between homosexuals and heterosexuals are foregrounded. The priority here is to limit the operations of Queteletian normativity by asserting similarity and averting the nearly inevitable interpretation of differences as deficiency.

Second, by emphasizing *stigma* as a social cause of differences, the resolution recognized 'homophobia' and related topics as legitimate psychological concerns. The term 'stigma' was a sociological one, elaborated by Erving Goffman in the previous decade by drawing on numerous symbolic interactionist sociology studies that described how people managed 'spoiled identities' and the responses that they invoked.[21] In contrast, only *discrimination*, but not the psychology of *stigma* was mentioned in the earlier statement by the Board of Trustees of the American Psychiatric Association.[22] This difference between psychologists and psychiatrists would remain pivotal, and the generation of knowledge about stigma and prejudice would become central *only* to psychology in the decades that followed.

Finally, the American Psychological Association's resolution called for action to oppose stigma *within* the profession, addressing itself to 'all mental health professionals.' By urging mental health professionals to act, the resolution provided a rationale for actions that would reverse the empirical gaze towards psychological experts, as Hooker's experiment had done. But at the same time, the resolution undercut the sentiments of authors such as Kameny who argued that mental health professionals and psychological research were irrelevant. As Kitzinger's work made clear later in the 1980s, the view that psychology was *irrelevant* to social change continued to seem 'radical.' Psychologists could admit that they should change more quickly than admit that they were unimportant.

One way to change a paradigm is to take stock of its questions and propose alternatives. Psychologist Stephen Morin, a member of BSERP's Task Force on the Status of Lesbian and Gay Male Psychologists, reviewed the contents of research studies kept in the APA's comprehensive archive of *Psychological Abstracts* published 1967–1974.[23] Morin cataloged 170 research questions that psychologists had asked in 139 studies, and categorized them into five groups. For example, on thirteen occasions researchers had asked questions about attitudes toward homosexuality, as mentioned above. These were 'the clearest example of research that is on the offense rather than the defense with regard to the advancement of gay civil liberties.'[24] Among the 139 studies, many more concerned men than women.

The most commonly asked research question concerned homosexuality's cause. Morin shared Kameny's scepticism about research into this question. Four paradigms had been brought to bear: behavioral studies which assumed homosexuality was a learned erotic response; psychoanalytic theories which assumed homosexuality was rooted in parent–child psychodynamics; endocrine theories which investigated effects of hormones on the brain; and ethological theories drawing on observations of animals. Among these four, only the few ethological studies asked the causal question in a way that was not tied to the agenda of turning gay people straight. (Although Morin did not say so, no psychologist had yet questioned why people become heterosexual.) Two related clusters of research questions focused on whether or not homosexuals could be 'adjusted' (or were always sick by definition) and how to *detect* a homosexual. Morin critiqued studies on adjustment for using small arbitrary samples. Attempts to detect homosexuals had often used projective tests, like the Rorschach, and had been often tied to the goal of *diagnosing* homosexuality.

The final category was 'special topics,' which were concerned with 'unique aspects in the lives of lesbians and gay men': coming out and self-disclosure, aging, relationships, social support, and involvement in subcultures. This category occupied about one-fifth of the literature and Morin predicted it would grow in the coming years. To overcome 'heterosexist bias,' researchers would need to question assumptions about representativeness, select research questions relevant to lesbians' and gay men's lives, and continue research on special topics and on the meaning of attitudes. Morin was optimistic that the new *Journal of Homosexuality* and *Homosexual Counselling Journal*, which both began publication in 1974, would foster such research.

Between Morin's 1977 review and Laura Brown's presidential address, psychologists increasingly used Kuhn's notion of the paradigm shift to explain historical change in the field.[25] Morin did not refer to Kuhnian paradigm shifts as Brown later did, but was calling for a paradigm shift and outlining its promise. Moreover his review set something of a paradigm for how to conceptualize the psychological research literature on lesbians and gay men that others emulated. Alan Watters repeated Morin's analysis by examining 166 psychological studies published 1979–1983.[26] By this time, far fewer studies investigated the cause of homosexuality, and virtually none considered adjustment or detection. 'Special topics' now comprised 56% of the literature and the proportion of the literature devoted to attitudes and prejudice had doubled. Morin's predicted and called-for paradigm shift happened in one decade.

Kuhn's popularity among psychologists was a consequence not only of his borrowings from early cognitive psychology, but also of a certain vagueness as to whether a paradigm shift is a shift between equally valid ways of conceptualizing reality or a shift from a worse to a better framework. Such calls for change allow you to critique the present in the absence of specifying how to deal with the problems that your new paradigm might introduce.[27] (In the interests of transparency, let me admit that I have not always been above doing this myself.)[28] In rejecting questions about causality, adjustment, and detection, Morin's understanding of heterosexist bias rejected *all* research that examined differences, helping to explain why Brown could later see a focus on normative creativity as a break with an established paradigm. At times, he missed the promise of affirmative research that was focused on difference. For example, like Evelyn Hooker, June Hopkins had engaged with the Rorschach inkblot test, and drawn positive conclusions from her tests about the personalities of lesbians as a group. Morin (1977) categorized her work as research on diagnosis, but – like Hooker – Hopkins conducted her research with affirmative goals in mind, and she did so in collaboration with a lesbian group as Hooker did with the Mattachine Society.[29] Such normative creativity as Hopkins' was incommensurate with the new lesbian and gay psychology paradigm focused on similarities.

Researchers in the emerging paradigm also sometimes shied away from interpreting meaningful group differences when they observed them. The most notable growth in 'special topics' research in Watters' period was in the study of same-sex relationships. One survey published in the APA's prestigious *Journal of Personality and Social Psychology* would have reached a wide readership, and compared the power strategies used by students in same- and different-sex romantic relationships.[30] Those in same-sex relationships reported greater desire for power in their relationships, and a greater belief that they possessed it. The authors made little of this group difference, even though social psychologists increasingly theorized perceived equality in relationships as central to their success by the late 1970s.[31] This group difference could have been – but was not – interpreted as a positive difference, a kind of 'normative creativity' in these relationships.

External events explain why such group differences were rarely prioritized. To illustrate, consider the situations of many married women who came out as lesbian in the 1970s. Lesbians routinely faced child custody threats from their ex-husbands, particularly if and when their lesbianism was discovered. Lesbian parents were adaptive in the 'creativity directed toward the complexities of negotiating identity' in this context. For some, coming out disrupted traditional kinship, some experienced pressure to have more normal families, and others to raise their daughters as 'little Amazons.' In one study, 41% of lesbian mothers had experienced or been threatened by such battles.[32] The Lesbian Mothers National Defense Fund was one early source of collective support.[33] Geraldine Cole, one of the group's co-founders, later recalled that in court 'You had to be a perfect mother. You couldn't be an average mother and you couldn't make mistakes. And people did make mistakes – and at that point they would lose in court all the time.'[34] In 1973, Bruce Voeller, president of the Gay Activist Alliance, solicited expert judgment from several psychologists and doctors to confirm that lesbians and gay men could parent. Mental health professionals were supportive of individual lesbians' custody cases. In 1975, the APA Council of Representatives adopted a resolution that 'the sex, gender identity, or sexual orientation of natural or prospective adoptive or foster parents should not be the sole or primary variable considered in custody or placement cases.'[35] By the end of the 1970s, parenting cases were increasingly supported by the Lesbian Rights Project in San Francisco and the ACLU.[36]

Psychiatrist Richard Green defended lesbian parents by subjecting them to the psychiatric gaze and finding evidence of no difference. Ironically, his battery of tests included the *projective* draw-a-person test to assess children's sexual and gender identity, and his defense of lesbian mothers relied on the extent to which their children's genders were normative and their sexualities appeared to be heterosexual.[37] Other researchers adopted similar strategies where lesbian mothers faced threats to maintaining child custody.[38] This work most clearly shows the thinking in the 1972 NIMH Task Force Report and the American Psychiatric Association resolution: adult lesbians' parenting rights were being protected from legal discrimination, but in a way that conceded that the promotion of homosexuality in future generations was unthinkable. As such, lesbian mothers were protected to an extent that would seem far from progressive if applied to many other minority groups. By so doing, such research communicated a prejudice, a prejudgment about the value of homosexuality.

From homophobia to heterosexism

Homophobia was not in short supply for those who wished to study it. The National Opinion Research Center at the University of Chicago had carried out the General Social Survey in most years between 1972 and 1994 and every two years since 1994.[39] Since the 1970s, the GSS has asked respondents whether the civil liberties of homosexuals should be protected and whether or not 'sexual relations between two adults of the same sex' is 'always wrong,' 'almost always wrong,' 'sometimes wrong,' 'not wrong at all,' 'other,' or 'don't know.' Troubling contemporary stereotypes about the permissive 1970s, the percentage of respondents who gave one of the last two 'permissive' responses increased only modestly from 19% to 22.4% from 1972 to 1978, inducing little optimism among the researchers that heterosexual prejudice was on the decline.[40]

The assumption that beliefs in group differences evidenced heterosexist bias influenced the concept of *homophobia* also. In Kuhnian terms, homophobia research was in something of a pre-paradigm-shift state in the late 1970s; researchers independently developed several questionnaires that made incommensurate assumptions about what homophobia and homosexuality were. Through a clever reading of individual items that were written for inclusion on these attitude measures, Celia Kitzinger detected a 'liberal humanist' ideology at work. Psychologists deemed agreement with statements that homosexual and heterosexual groups were *similar*, that homosexuals were diverse rather than politically unified, that homosexuality was natural rather than chosen, and that lesbians and gay men posed no threat to the larger heterosexual society as evidence of *non-prejudiced* attitude.[41] Kitzinger further noted that all of those beliefs were antithetical to a radical lesbian feminist position which politicized lesbian identity and considered it distinctly superior to choosing the heterosexual alternative.

Later Sean Massey and I revisited these early scales, noting that they tended to take the 'homosexuality' that homophobia opposed to have a wider range of meanings than later scales did. On these early measures, the homosexuality in question included gay/lesbian individuals, their politics, and their sexual behavior. On occasion, discomfort with homosexuality in oneself, particularly among men, was deemed a sign of homophobia. For example, Mosher and O'Grady's measure of *homosexual threat* asked male participants to assess their agreement or disagreement with items referring to same-sex eroticism and desire, such as 'to love another man is to know the heights of the human soul' and 'I could never bring myself to suck another man's cock.'[42] Such items could just as readily be seen as measuring *biphobia* directly towards the self as *homophobia* directed towards others.[43] Although there was some study of bisexual-identified people's lives and interests in the 1970s, they did not influence the paradigm emerging in psychology for some time, and such measures were understood as being clearly about *homophobia*.[44]

Watters' review noted thirty-six new studies on social attitudes, and many more of these were published beyond specialist venues; attitudes research reached psychology's mainstream before other 'special topics' research. Going beyond surveys, researchers had begun to conduct *experimental* studies on the effects of labeling a person as gay or straight on others' memory, evaluations, and emotional responses.[45] Once again, paradigmatic assumptions can be detected in retrospect. Experiments on the effects of labeling were interpreted as showing different treatment of people who *are* homosexual, but in reality they often required people to interact with the same person, or to anticipate meeting an imaginary person, who was described as gay or straight. The experiments could not only be read as showing discrimination along group identity lines, but also the consequences for social interaction of coming out, or having others out you.

Prejudice research became more paradigmatic in the 1980s, particularly through the work of social psychologist Gregory Herek.[46] Herek insisted on the term 'heterosexism' because the prejudice in question was a form of group prejudice like sexism or racism, and not a pathological *phobic* response. He also developed the Attitudes Toward Lesbians and Gay Men Scale, a one-dimensional measure of social attitudes ranging from *condemnation* to *tolerance* of lesbians and gay men. Herek described how heterosexism served diverse functions, including *experiential* functions drawing on experiences with lesbians and gay men, such *symbolic* functions as the expression of group membership, and *ego-defensive* functions, such as those that concerned Mosher and O'Grady. Although the functional explanation of social attitudes was somewhat out of vogue in social psychology in the 1980s, Herek used it effectively to unify and simplify the measurement of *heterosexism* whilst also opening up multiple reasons to investigate its diverse causes. He became the most prolific author in lesbian and gay psychology and a key organizer within the field from the mid-1980s onward.

Counseling and the good life

Lesbian and gay psychology also fit particularly well with the humanistic ethos of *counseling* psychology in the period of depathologization and afterwards. Counseling psychology had its origins in rehabilitation of soldiers after World War II but in the 1960s, under the influence of figures such as Carl Rogers, counseling psychology emerged as a third wave in American psychology aimed at the affirmation of human potential rather than psychodynamic working or the control of behavior.[47] Indeed, the first openly gay-affirmative symposium at the American Psychological Association was organized in 1973, under the auspices of the Division for Humanistic Psychology.[48] Many of the early members of the BSERP's Task Force on the Status of Lesbian and Gay Male Psychologists were active in the formulation of lesbian and gay-affirmative helping professions beyond the APA. Barbara Sang co-founded the Homosexual Community Counseling Center in New York City in 1971, and Harold Kooden was a founding member of the National Gay and Lesbian Health Foundation.[49] There was an obvious fit between lesbian and gay psychologists' aims and claims and the Rogerian values of listening to others without judgment, offering unconditional positive regard to others, and working to empower individuals to transcend socially imposed constraints to reach their full potential. Robin Buhrke and her colleagues made a survey of counseling psychology research from 1978 to 1989 using Morin's categories. They found an exclusively affirmative focus; researchers showed no interest in questions about the causes, detection, or 'adjustment' of gay men and lesbians.[50]

Two theoretical developments originating within counseling psychology in the 1980s have had particularly lasting effects on lesbian and gay psychology: stage models of identity and the explanation of identity failures as effects of *internalized* homophobia. I examine their developments and critics next. Stage models of identity picked up a tradition of mapping distinct challenges to adult 'life stages' more ancient than psychology, but most prominently developed in psychology by Erik Erikson.[51] Erikson's theory was emblematic of a trend in American psychology in the generation after World War II. Such theories presumed that individuals had greater capacity to resolve psychological conflicts than darker Freudian models had done. Because they are offered as general guides to the good life, such theories as Erikson's can quickly shift from descriptions to Galtonian ideals of how life should or must be lived to constitute a good life. In so doing, such theories can easily take insufficient account of how social contexts limit individuals' capacities or complicate their desires to live life in the ways that these theories describe as desirable, healthy, or mature. For this reason, Erikson's theory included generalizations about gender differences that became an immediate target for early feminist psychologists.[52] Informed by his experiences in the Black Power movement, psychologist William Cross developed a completely different stage model specific to the ways in which a Black identity is formulated. This model specifies the formation of identity by transcending the socialization that minimizes the importance of Black identity, that is prompted by encounters that make a racialized world view pressing, through a stage of immersion/emersion when Black identity feels like it must be proven, until Black identity is successfully internalized, and ultimately accepted along with the racial identities of others.[53]

Cross' model formed one basis for early models of what the 'coming out process' might look like for lesbians and gay men. His paper on his model is the first reference cited by the most influential model of the coming out process, authored by Australian counseling psychologist Vivienne Cass. Like Cross', Cass' model posited six stages. *Identity confusion* was initiated by the perception that information about homosexuality is self-relevant. During *identity comparison* the individual forms explanations of their homosexual feelings. *Identity tolerance* makes contact with other homosexuals pressing. When these contacts lead homosexuality to be normalized, *identity acceptance* has been reached. Heterosexual others are actively devalued during *identity pride*, until *identity synthesis* occurs, when 'the "them and us" philosophy espoused previously, in which all heterosexuals are viewed negatively and all homosexuals positively, no longer holds true.'[54] Cross and his colleagues have extensively revised and updated his model in subsequent decades to incorporate the rise of multicultural identities, concern for the normative implications of positing some adult identities as more developed than others, and the distinction between personal and social identity.[55] Cass' model required similar revisions. For example, although inspired by models of Black identity development, her model did not take account of the complexity of forming Black gay identities in social contexts marked by both racist and homophobic exclusion.[56] Cass also described bisexual identity as something that is passed through early on, on the way to a more mature gay or lesbian identity. Although some people do have this experience, the model afforded this interpretation as the only or most typical reason for a person to identify as bisexual.

As Katherine Johnson's excellent recent discussion of the development of sexual identity models since Cass details, historical shifts in available minority identities and concerns about the normalizing implications of identity theories have stalked this literature from the beginning.[57] Revisions and additions to identity models have typically been far more explicit about the excluded identity narratives that they rightly champion than about how they repeat the identity paradigm that created such exclusions in the first place. As such, the accumulation of identity models converges on the limits of individualist analysis itself, the impossibility of answering the question of how to live an individual 'good life' without also saying that some lives are better than others. There is an inevitable risk that describing the good life for those who have been denied such descriptions can create new social norms that also exclude.

Counseling psychologists also described explicitly what the *failure* of healthy identity development looked like. Lesbians and gay men did not always respond to counseling psychologists' interventions and the familiar concept of *internalized homophobia* was invoked to explain lesbians and gay men who did not engage and access services, alcoholism, and difficulties in coming out.[58] Internalized homophobia did not fit Morin's original scheme, as it located the *origin* of distress in society, but also describes those dynamics as having a life of their own *internal* to the lesbian or gay individual's psyche. For this reason, Kitzinger critiqued this construct as re-pathologizing lesbians who failed to comply with psychologists' norms.[59] Although she didn't say so, her critique sits within a larger set of concerns about how ideas about self-hatred are used to create conformity to noxious political positions: White supremacist leaders court followers by calling on White people to overcome their internalized self-hatred.[60] This criticism remains relevant because internalized homophobia has expanded from its origins in counseling and is now often measured in research on sexual minorities. By the early years of the twenty-first century a full quarter of the psychological literature on homophobia, heterosexism, or sexual prejudice was about *internalized* homophobia.[61]

Internalized homophobia was also relevant because lesbians and gay men could, by their own volition, continue to appeal to mental health professionals for help in changing their sexual orientation. Measures of internalized homophobia often asked lesbians, gay men, and bisexual people about such wishes. In the early 1970s, 'ex-gay' ministries such as Love in Action and Exodus International began to emerge from the counter culture, and ministries reworked a different logic of personal experience, circulating conversion narratives of coming out *of homosexuality* rather than *as* lesbian or gay.[62] In 1980, the *DSM-III* included the category 'ego-dystonic homosexuality.' This diagnosis was removed from the revised *DSM-III (DSM III-R)* of 1987 but means of diagnosing homosexuality remained.[63] Such diagnostic possibilities squared the demands of traditional psychiatric normalization and the calls to respect lesbians' and gay men's claim to be experts on their own experiences.

The influence of this diagnosis and its prioritizing of *individual self-determination* over opposition to societal homophobia is evident in the Report on an important survey of practitioner psychologists completed in 1986 by an APA Task Force of the Committee on Lesbian Gay and Concerns (CLGC), a group that I will describe in the next chapter. The responses of 2,544 APA members reported on incidents where therapists had either provided inadequate care or shown 'special sensitivity' to gay or lesbian clients. Mirroring other findings that lesbians and gay men remained active consumers of psychotherapy after depathologization, 99% of psychologists reported having had at least one lesbian or gay client, and 58% reported negative incidents with such clients. In the CLGC Report, many psychologists described as bad practice those cases where psychologists urged clients to give up same-sex behaviors or gay or lesbian identities. However, the authors also singled out as *exemplary practice* a therapist who assisted 'a male client who expressed a strong desire to "go straight."' This incident, its reporting on the survey, and its categorization as exemplary practice all attest to Kitzinger's thesis that psychology's commitment to *the self-determining individual* limited the extent to which it could promise structural readjustments beyond psychiatric normalization.

Open season on gay kids

The focus of lesbian and gay-affirmative psychology on adults represents one of its foundational limits and one with which the field still wrestles. The Report of the NIMH Task Force stated:

> For most workers in the field, prevention of the development of a homosexual orientation is seen as one of the most important goals. In light of this, intensive effort should be made to understand better the factors involved in effective primary prevention. It is apparent that research in a number of the areas described above, including parental relationships, childhood peer

activities, endocrine, genetic and biological elements, effects of early trauma, the role of social class mores, and developmental crises will have a direct bearing on the design of preventive programs.[64]

The force of sexual liberationist claims to speak truth from experience were also limited in regard to how to think about *children*, and 'the child' is one of the central objects of modern psychology and one through which fantasies about normalization operate forcefully.[65] Children are not so easily recognized as political subjects in liberal humanist discourse that relies on speaking from experience, particularly as sexual subjects.[66] Two consequences of the split impulse to affirm adult lesbians and gay men whilst seeking new ways to prevent homosexuality in future generations have already been described. First, the contingent affirmation of parents of diverse sexualities and genders was premised on the gender and sexual normalcy of their children, and second, the affirmation of adult lesbian and gay identities was contingent upon moving through a series of intelligible developmental stages toward 'mature' identities..

The Report gave new reasons to animate heterosexist bias in the prevention of homosexuality in the young. In the 1970s, the proportion of adult lesbians and gay men who might approach psychiatrists for treatment of their 'sexual orientation disturbance' was very low. The proportion of parents who sought professional help in the best interests of their children who showed signs of early queerness grew. The NIMH Report gave full backing to the expansion of psychiatry to respond to, if not to address, such parents' anxieties.[67] In 1971, psychiatrist Richard Green founded the International Academy of Sex Research (IASR), and he edited its journal *Archives of Sexual Behavior* until 2001. Then and now, *Archives* was a firmly empiricist journal, and the IASR strongly identified as a professional, and somewhat elite, body. *Archives* continued discussion of questions about homosexuality's causes and adjustment, drawing on studies of intersex children to debate the influences of learning and foetal hormones as causes of homosexuality, evaluating treatments of homosexuality, and weighing up the relationship between homosexuality and psychopathy.[68] I do not mean that the authors writing here clung rigidly to the diagnostic view of homosexuality, only that they continued to engage empirical questions that defined heterosexist bias for Morin.

Gender, not sexuality, was the central focus in this journal, and many of its authors wrote from gender identity clinics and debated in pre-paradigm-shift fashion the definitions, detection, causes, and treatments of transsexual people. Mental health professionals were keen to construct explanations, whether based on biology, psychoanalysis, or learning theory, that might explain and justify sex realignment. Heteronormativity shaped the practices that informed this research literature; people were considered good candidates for treatment to the extent that they would conform to heterosexuality afterward.[69] These debates became somewhat more paradigmatic following the publication of the Harry Benjamin International Gender Dysphoria Association's Standards of Care in 1979 and the diagnosis of Transsexualism in the *DSM-III*.[70]

Archives also provided a forum for discussion of the nature and treatment of children who showed strong interest in the identities and interests of a gender other than the one assigned at birth. As Karl Bryant has documented, Robert Spitzer was the primary architect of *DSM-III* and he invited Richard Green to author a new diagnosis of Gender Identity Disorder in Childhood around 1975 that would capture a description of such children.[71] Spitzer hoped that the *DSM-III* would move away from controversies created by assumptions about the causes of psychiatric illness, and quiet the critics that psychiatry had gathered in previous decades. The *DSM-III* included the new diagnoses of Gender Identity Disorder in Childhood defined by two criteria: cross-gender identification and persistent and intense distress about being assigned as a boy or as a girl.

Green was certainly the most successful researcher who studied these children in the 1970s. Since the mid-1950s, Green, under the tutelage of John Money and Robert Stoller, had studied children being raised as boys who expressed desires to live as girls. In the late 1960s, he began a longitudinal 'Study of the Development of Atypical Sex Roles in Children,' mostly boys, recruited through the UCLA gender identity clinic, and supported by approximately $400,000 in NIMH grants between 1973 and 1979. This was a sizeable chunk of the NIMH funding available; the total of all NIH funding for research in *all* health research in all health fields about homosexuality over the period 1974–1981 was only $3.3 million. When 'a cranky NIMH project reviewer' disrupted the flow of cash to Green's project, the Playboy Foundation filled the gap.[72] From the 1980s onward, Green's grant was titled in a manner consistent with the newly created diagnosis of GIDC as 'Gender Identity Development: Atypical and Typical' and remained funded by NIMH. Green wrote his book at Stanford's prestigious Center for the Advanced Study of Behavioral Sciences, following nomination by psychiatrist Edwin Shneidman, a friend of Evelyn Hooker's who had acted as one of the 'blind' judges in her original study.[73]

Bryant documents how gay organizations in psychology and psychiatry were not at all consulted on the drafting of this diagnosis. However, the diagnosis became available to the APA Committee on Women, who objected strongly to its conflation of gender identity confusion with tomboyism.[74] Since its inception in *DSM-III*, the diagnosis has always been applied far more often to children assigned as boys than to those assigned as girls. Feminist psychologists had less obvious ontological reasons to take issue with the diagnosis than the understandable wish to shelter tomboys from it.

Personality psychologists had long assumed – without empirical evidence – that to be 'masculine' was to be 'not feminine' by definition and vice versa. Feminist psychologist Anne Constantinople made clear in a critical review in 1973 that the rationale for psychologists to designate any human behavior as 'masculine' or 'feminine' was unclear at best in the literature on personality, and that the detection of male homosexuality had been a repeated rationale for developing such measures in the first place.[75] In the early 1970s, feminist psychologists initiated a paradigm shift with new measures of 'sex roles' that allowed the possibility that a woman or a man could be both highly masculine *and* highly feminine, and valorized those individuals with 'androgynous' personalities who could adapt flexibly to any social situation.[76] In contrast, the questionnaire measures of gender *identity* introduced in *Archives* in the 1970s, and applied in gender identity clinics, crystalized that the diagnosis of Gender Identity Disorder itself assumed a single masculinity–femininity axis. In feminist psychology of the 1970s, androgyny was often seen as a sign of flexibility and psychological health. In the Gender Identity Clinics, gender had a more rigid ontology, psychological masculinity and femininity were required to be opposites of each other, and the conditions for recognizing gender fluidity as healthy or creative were profoundly more limited.[77]

The treatment of children whose genders brought them to clinical attention also incited public criticism for causing more harm than good. The program at UCLA, which Green directed, and from which he drew his participants, was exposed and critiqued in an article in *Rolling Stone* magazine and in later publications.[78] For example, one child treated by psychologist George Rekers and behavior therapist Ivan Lovaas, identified as 'Kraig,' was in treatment for half a year. His behavioral program extended beyond the administration of rewards and punishments for gender-typed and gender cross-typed behaviors in the clinic to the tutelage of his parents in how to dole out economies of reward and punishment in the home.[79] In short, the treatment constituted a sort of psychological rationale for amplifying the homophobic anxieties that led his parents to bring children such as Kraig to the clinic in the first place.[80]

By the mid-1970s, leaders of the American Association for Behavior Therapy had spoken out against its use in treating homosexuality, *even if* such treatments were effective,[81] and there were occasional clashes between the psychological affirmative paradigm and the psychiatric paradigm in regard to such children. In his review, Morin queried the politics of NIMH's decision to fund research on preventing homosexuality in children.[82] In a letter of response published in *American Psychologist*, George Rekers attacked Morin's objectivity, describing his attribution of *heterosexist bias* to researchers interested in the cause, detection, and prevention of homosexuality as 'confounding values and science, albeit in the opposite direction of past researchers.'[83] Rekers transparently stated that *he* considered homosexual behavior morally sinful, and argued for continuing research identifying children 'at risk' of transsexualism, transvestism, and homosexuality, such as Kraig, with prevention in mind. Rekers and Morin also exchanged blows in 1978 in a special issue of the *Journal of Social Issues*, over the issue of parental consent to such treatment, with Rekers and his colleagues supporting parents' rights to impose homophobic moral standards on their children, whilst Morin and Schultz argued that the recognition of gay rights required the protection of children from attempts to stamp out homosexuality in developing children.[84] This debate is rarely remembered, but its terms are far from settled in the present.

As often happens in psychology, ethical and political debate were somewhat muted by new empirical observations. In 1981 Kinsey Institute researchers Bell, Weinberg, and Hammersmith published the book-length study *Sexual Preference: Its Development in Women and Men*, one of several reports of an NIMH-funded investigation into the social organization of homosexuality carried out in the late 1960s.

Sexual Preference distilled the results of hundreds of structured interviews about life experiences with gay, lesbian, bisexual, and straight, White and Black women and men, linking developmental events in childhood to later adult sexualities. With its large samples gathered outside of clinical contexts, its use of a heterosexual control group and statistical path models, *Sexual Preference* seemed to make a robust contribution to the question of homosexuality's causes.

The book hit the zeitgest to which *DSM-III* oriented. It made little mention of the tumultuous climate of the late 1960s when the data were collected and in which gay liberationist protests of psychiatry originated, and it reported little statistical support for the now-rejected psychoanalytic theories that rested on differences in parenting. It also made the pre-homosexual child a figure about which the psychiatric questions about detection, adjustment, and change could continue to circulate. The researchers found that adult women and *particularly* adult men were less likely to be heterosexual if they reported 'feeling different' as children and preferred playmates and interests not prescribed for their gender. Moreover, such children were far less likely to report having playmates and interests characteristic of the gender to which they were assigned at birth. To be sure, this link between children's genders and adult sexualities was statistically stronger among lesbian and gay than bisexual respondents, stronger among White than Black respondents, and stronger among women who had been in therapy. These interactions did not deter authors from drawing on this study, along with Green's *longitudinal* study of the children in the UCLA clinic, to assert the hypothesis of a universal causal relationship between childhood gender nonconformity and adult homosexuality in both psychology and psychiatry.

In the early 1980s, under Green's continued editorship, *Archives* became the primary site for debating the strengths of hormonal and learning theory as explanations of this link between childhood gender and adult sexuality. Green was disappointed that his hopes to have detected those children most likely to grow up to be transsexual had not borne fruit. Instead, many of the children that he studied through the UCLA gender identity clinic grew up to identify as gay or bisexual men. As its title suggests, Green's *The Sissy Boy Syndrome and the Development of Homosexuality* is deliberately unknowing about the fact that psychiatrists' language has performative effects – and can do things, such as *insult, silence,* or *trouble* the people that it describes. In an insightful critique of Green's and other psychiatrists' work, Eve Sedgwick noted that 'affirmation' in the helping professions was limited to gay men who were masculine adults.[85] Sedgwick noted the repeated assumptions that boys' effeminacy equated to ill-health in Green's book, and that boys require a stable masculine core gender identity. Describing Green's book as 'a tissue of lies to children about their parents' motives for bringing them in', Sedgwick noted that psychiatrists validate parents' homophobic motives to protect their children, and raised concerns about the effects of teasing peers. At one point, Green also identified such teasing itself as 'natural therapy' by virtue of its punishing effects and the possibility that it might inculcate more 'masculine' behavior. Such psychiatric writings show that neither the feminist celebration of androgynous sex roles, nor the affirmation of lesbian and gay adults had undone the exercise of Queteletian normalization on children, which remained focused on those who stubbornly refused to confirm that idiom that 'boys will be boys.'

Sedgwick was right that Green's scheme stretched the meaning of affirmation to render it meaningless, and did so precisely because it assumed that a stable masculine identity is a requirement of gay men's mental health. But she stopped short of critiquing *Sexual Preference*, which she described as singularly credible and gay-affirmative. I am not so sure, in large part because of conducting controlled psychological experiments about how people interpret the results of studies that yield group differences. In 1997–1998, I conducted studies in which I presented undergraduates with the results of such retrospective recall studies as *Sexual Preference* or the results of bogus studies in which heterosexual people recall more gender nonconforming childhood experiences than their lesbian/gay counterparts. I asked the students to explain the studies' results in their own words. In my research, students' explanations assumed these childhood differences to be real if they had been presented with findings like those in *Sexual Preference*. However, if they were presented with counter-stereotype findings, participants were more likely to attribute the group differences to gay and lesbian people's memory distortions and lies to the interviewers.

Regardless of which pattern of results was presented, many more students explained why lesbian or gay development was different from heterosexual development than the reverse. In *Sexual Preference* itself, gay/lesbian development is also persistently described in terms of its difference from heterosexual development, such that heterosexual development is never positioned as something that needs an explanation. This habit of thinking, in the experiments and in the volume, is not intentional; the authors of *Sexual Preference* introduce their volume by critiquing studies that contrast the development of homosexuality 'against a backdrop of stereotypic untested assumptions about heterosexuals' (p. xi). However, these patterns of explanation can have consequences, as they implicitly signal to people who read them which group is the norm and has power, agency, and worth.[86]

Whilst most authors assumed the results of *Sexual Preference* to be valid, a few contested whether people would re-construct their childhood experiences on the basis of their adult sexual identities.[87] None raised the question whether heterosexual people's gender identities could be built upon the repudiation of homosexuality from the outset, rendering them a non-neutral standard for any comparison. Consequently, Sedgwick's important critique misses subtle forms of heteronormativity in *Sexual Preference*, and misses the critical potentiation opened up when experiments reverse the gaze from questions about group differences to the assumptions that ground those questions. Sedgwick's criticisms of Green give a sense that affirmation remained partial and precarious, particularly in regard to children, explaining why Laura Brown was moved in 1988 to call for something more transformative than the existing lesbian/gay psychology, why that call appeared novel, and why it seemed to many to be too terrifying and exhilarating to answer.

Notes

1 Kuhn (1970).
2 Kameny (1997 [1965], pp. 338–339). See also Kameny (2009).
3 Pickren & Schneider (2005).
4 See Minton (2002, p. 237).
5 See Bayer (1981) for a fuller history of these events.
6 Fort, Steiner, & Conrad (1971); Gartrell, Kraemer, & Brodie (1974).
7 Milgram (1974). On behavior therapy controversies see Rutherford (2009).
8 Davison & Wilson (1973).
9 Weinberg (1972, p. 1).
10 See Crandall, Eshleman, & O'Brien (2002).
11 This figure is drawn from Morin (1977), and the first intervention reported was Morin (1974). The first study was Smith (1971).
12 Faderman (1991).
13 Rich (1980). For an example of theory critiqued by Rich, see Chodorow (1978).
14 Wittig (1992, 'The Straight Mind').
15 See Brown (2006, February 4).
16 Pickren & Tomes (2002).
17 Meara & Myers (1999, p. 33).
18 Kimmel & Browning (1999, pp. 131–132).
19 Conger (1975, p. 633).
20 See www.apa.org/pi/lgbt/resources/policy/
21 Goffman (1963).
22 The resolution read as follows 'The American Psychiatric Association deplores all public and private discrimination against homosexuals in such areas as employment, housing, public accommodation, and licensing, and declares that no burden of proof shall be placed upon homosexuals greater than that imposed on any other persons. Further, the American Psychiatric Association supports and urges the enactment of civil rights legislation at the local, state, and federal level that would offer homosexual citizens the same protections now guaranteed to others on the basis of race, creed, color, etc. Further, the American Psychiatric Association supports and urges repeal of all discriminatory legislation singling out homosexual acts by consenting adults in private' American Psychiatric Association (1974).
23 Morin (1977).
24 Morin (1977, p. 635).
25 Driver-Linn (2003).
26 Watters (1986).
27 Driver-Lynn (2003).
28 Hegarty (2009a).
29 Hubbard and Hegarty (2016).
30 Falbo & Peplau (1980).
31 See Walster, Walster, & Berscheid (1978).
32 Lewin (1993, see p. 182).
33 Rivers (2010).
34 See excerpt from oral history with Geraldine Cole here: http://outhistory.org/exhibits/show/queen-city-comes-out/community-organizations/lmndf. Downloaded August 15, 2016.
35 www.apa.org/about/policy/custody-placement.pdf
36 Rivers (2010, p. 932).
37 See Green (1982).
38 See Golombok et al. (1983), Kirkpatrick et al. (1981).
39 Davis & Smith (1992).
40 Glenn & Weaver (1979, p. 109).

41 Kitzinger (1987).
42 Mosher & O'Grady (1979).
43 Hegarty & Massey (2006).
44 Blumstein & Schwartz (1976, 1977), Klein (1979), Storms (1979).
45 See e.g., Cuenot & Fugita (1982).
46 See particularly Herek (1984, 1986a, 1986b, 1987).
47 Rogers (1961).
48 Kimmel & Browning (1999, p. 131).
49 See Barbara Sang's oral history here: http://herstories.prattinfoschool.nyc/omeka/collections/show/60. Downloaded June 18, 2016.
50 Buhrke et al. (1992).
51 Erikson (1959, 1964).
52 See for example Weisstein (1971).
53 Cross (1971).
54 Cass (1979, p. 234).
55 See Cross (1991), Vandiver et al. (2002), Worrell et al. (2001).
56 Icard (1986), Loiacano (1989).
57 Johnson (2015).
58 See Malyon (1982); Messing et al. (1984), Finnegan and Cook (1984) and Lourea (1985).
59 Kitzinger (1987).
60 Finlay (2005, 2007).
61 Hegarty (2006).
62 Erzen (2006).
63 Zucker and Spitzer (2005).
64 NIMH (1969, p. 5) Task Force on Homosexuality.
65 Burman (2008).
66 Pateman (1988).
67 My use of the term queer here is intended to signal that such children were brought to the attention of professionals because of visible difference that was an ambiguous signifier of transsexualism and homosexuality. My use of the term is not an anachronistic projection of queer theory back in time; 'queer' has been used to describe psychologists' fears about difference in children, including that linked to gender and sexual difference, at least since the original work of psychologist Lewis Terman (Hegarty, 2013). Indeed, I mean the term here to establish a genealogy between Terman's work, the continuation of its assumptions in psychiatry, biology, and sexology in the 1970s, and its critiques from within the lesbian and gay and feminist paradigms that emerged in psychology and elsewhere.
68 On causes of homosexuality drawing on intersex see Meyer-Bahlburg (1977), Money & Ehrhardt (1971), and Reinisch (1974). On treatments and adjustment of homosexuality see Adelman (1977), McConaghy, Proctor, & Barr (1972), Phillips, Fischer, & Groves (1976).
69 Bolin (1988).
70 Meyerowitz (2004 [1980]).
71 Bryant (2006).
72 See Green (1987, pp. ix–x), Burke (1996, p. 257), Silvestre (1999).
73 See Green (1987, p. x). Hooker (1993).
74 Bryant (2006, p. 32).
75 Constantinople (1973), Lewin (1984a, 1984b).
76 Bem (1974). See Hegarty (2003) on the valorization of androgyny.
77 Freund et al. (1974).
78 Bryant (2006).
79 See Rekers & Lovaas (1974). For later accounts see also Green (1987) and Burke (1996).

80 Burke (1996).
81 Davison (1976).
82 Morin (1977, p. 634).
83 Rekers (1978, p. 510).
84 Morin & Schultz (1978).
85 Sedgwick (1991).
86 Hegarty & Pratto (2001, 2004). The authors of *Sexual Preference* also explain how the Black participants differed from the White participants twice as often as they adopted the reverse frame of reference. For a review of this research including a discussion of the consequences of such asymmetric explanations see Hegarty & Bruckmüller (2013).
87 See particularly Ross (1980). On such reconstructive memory processes see also Carver et al. (2004).

3 Generalizing affirmation in the age of HIV/AIDS

The previous chapter examined the emergence of lesbian and gay-affirmative psychology. Here, I describe how these new affirmative views shifted from margin to center both through sustained organizing about lesbian and gay 'issues,' 'concerns,' and 'psychology,' and through the responses of psychologists to the HIV/AIDS epidemic in the 1980s. Like many fields of study, psychology was transformed by the complexity and urgency of the response required by the first decade of HIV/AIDS. Ordinary practices of peer-reviewing medical articles were suspended to accelerate the production of knowledge, and immunology became 'big science.'[1] One review of social work journals from 1988–1997 found that two-thirds of the studies on lesbian and gay issues focused on HIV/AIDS.[2] Historians approached AIDS with unusually urgent obligations to engage critically with unfolding historical events, drawing analogies to past epidemics and creating an 'AIDS effect' which had lasting effects on the history of recent medicine.[3] The HIV/AIDS epidemic required significant rupture in what counted as 'knowledge' in many disciplines.

Psychology was no different. HIV/AIDS was undoubtedly a 'lesbian and gay issue' and all were personally affected by it. But the centrality of HIV/AIDS in national health policy risked overwhelming other lesbian and gay concerns entirely. Funding for lesbian, gay, and bisexual research ran at about 5% of the total amount of funding for HIV/AIDS research in the 1980s.[4] HIV/AIDS also challenged the centrality of *identity* in understandings of sexuality. HIV was transmitted by sexual behavior, and prompted the need to think more flexibly about the ontological relationship between sexual behavior and sexual identity than this identity paradigm allowed.

The first decade of AIDS followed economic crises in the 1970s, as economic and political thinking coalesced around laissez-faire economic liberalism, particularly after President Ronald Reagan's election in 1980.[5] During the 1980s, social psychologists and policy makers increasingly turned to concepts such as self-esteem and self-efficacy to explain *individual differences* in managing life in this increasingly uncertain world. Kitzinger was not alone among critical psychologists to bemoan individualism in psychology, as new concepts such as 'employability' located capacities in persons and shifted risks and responsibilities for managing life away from states and corporations.[6] The new field of *health psychology* also oriented towards changing individuals' behaviors to manage national health issues, and changes in gay and bisexual men's sexual practices and in community norms in the early years of AIDS seemed to some to exemplify health psychology's promise. Like many agencies, the NIMH saw its budgets and programs slashed after Reagan's election, and funding for psychology fell accordingly.[7] Only in the later 1980s did the NIMH begin to fund more psychologists who were engaged in behavioral prevention of HIV transmission and other psychological responses to AIDS.

HIV/AIDS: the early years

In 1981, the US Center for Disease Control (CDC) first published accounts of clusters of gay men in Los Angeles and New York City with conditions that rarely affect young healthy people: the skin cancer Kaposi's sarcoma (KS) and pneumocystis pneumonia (PCP).[8] In a context in which the most established understanding of sex between men in American medicine was the psychiatric theory of homosexuality, these men and those who followed became objects of scientific and popular curiosity first, and people to care for only second. The first medical articles on 'immunocompromised homosexuals' appeared in 1981. The CDC set up a monitoring group with the 'surveillance definition' of the condition as Gay Related Immune Deficiency (GRID). In July 1983, psychologist readers of the newsletter *APA Monitor* would learn that of the 1522 people diagnosed with AIDS in the USA, 75% were homosexual men, 40% had died within a year, and 80% had died within two years.[9] The disease was understood as intrinsically gay and as deadly from the outset. Early theories attributed the epidemic to an 'immune overload' created by large numbers of sexual partners and recreational drug use, which were common among gay men. Even after clusters of cases were found among Haitian immigrants and haemophiliacs, and further cases were identified among heterosexual-identified people outside of these 'high-risk groups,' homosexuality continued to play a role in many minds as a factor that was causative of HIV/AIDS in and of itself. There are few social categories in which the default identity that people draw to mind is that of gay men, but over time the category of 'people with AIDS' became one.

Holistic responses to AIDS emerged slowly, partially, and first at local levels in the hardest hit cities. Organizations consisting mainly of gay men, such as Gay Men's Health Crisis in New York and the Kaposi's Sarcoma Research and Education Foundation (later renamed the San Francisco AIDS Foundation) initiated the first public health response to the epidemic. Among the most enduring impacts of this association of AIDS with gay men was the neglect of its impact on ethnic minorities. African-Americans have remained particularly over-represented in HIV statistics from the 1980s until today. As political scientist Cathy Cohen explains, Reagan's laissez-faire economic politics arrested and reversed processes by which people in Black communities were achieving political and economic power and representation over the 1970s. Black leaders also had many issues other than AIDS competing for attention and action in the early 1980s. HIV/AIDS not only appeared to be a White gay men's disease, but news of its occurrence in Black communities could be attributed to simple racism by some.[10]

The dilemmas created by individual behavior change as a response to the epidemic played out quickly in gay communities also. Theories that attributed the disease to lifestyle factors that might have led to an accumulation of 'stress' and immune breakdown incited heated ethical and political debate as to whether and how men ought to change their sexual practices. In August 1982, New York physician Lawrence Mass proposed a viral theory, and several teams of virologists investigated the hypothesis that the agent was a *retrovirus*. A retrovirus is a kind of virus with RNA genetic material, which contains the enzyme reverse transcriptase, and which reproduces by converting RNA to DNA. Based on the theory that people were getting sick because of a viral agent, two gay doctors, Callen and Berkowitz, published their manifesto *How to Have Sex in an Epidemic* in New York in 1983, asserting what we now call 'safe sex' as the way to respond to the epidemic. 'Safe sex' did not require avoiding anonymous sex or multiple partners, but minimizing the risk of transmission by using condoms. Berkowitz and Callen declared 'a war on the promiscuity' of 1970s, arguing that gay culture must evolve if that culture were to survive.[11]

The viral theory gathered strength. Luc Montagnier at the Pasteur Institute in Paris, France found reverse transcriptase in the enflamed lymph nodes of gay men in 1982, and in April 1983, Robert Gallo reported the discovery of the virus HTLV-III as a likely causal agent. Gallo assumed that Montagnier's virus was the same as his own. Montagnier insisted that it was not and identified his virus as LAV. In spite of considerable dispute regarding priority of discovery that I cannot do justice to here, on April 23, 1984, US Secretary of Health Margaret Hecker announced that the likely cause of HIV had been found. With rash ambition that alarmed the virologists, she further announced that a test for the virus was available and that a vaccine would be available within two years. The following month, the journal *Science* published four papers by the Gallo group claiming that the virus had been found, could be mass-produced, was related to Gallo's earlier HTLV-III, and that its antibodies could be detected in blood, allowing for testing. AIDS was declared the nation's top medical priority.

Early attempts to prompt the American Psychological Association towards a national response to HIV/AIDs were led by gay-affirmative psychologists, notably Stephen Morin. Discussion of HIV/AIDS within the APA was sometimes carried out 'quietly' because many members of APA resisted such discussions in the epidemic's early years. In 1982, under the auspices of BSERP, Morin wrote to the APA's Central Office raising concern about the impact of AIDS on the gay community and directing the APA to funding opportunities at the Center for Disease Control. His request was initially dismissed on the grounds that AIDS was a medical and not a psychological disease, but Morin continued to press the case. By 1983 the APA had begun to conceptualize existing research paradigms that could be brokered in the fight against AIDS, including research on the effects of stress on immune functioning. The Committee on Gay Concerns (COGC) urged that Walter Bachelor of the APA's Public Policy Office represent the APA nationally on AIDS and Bachelor worked with NIMH and other federal research agencies, becoming the APA's 'resident expert' on AIDS in the 1980s. In January 1984, the APA Council of Representatives accepted the recommendation of COGC to join FARO, the Federation of AIDS-Related Organizations.[12]

Bachelor edited a special section of *American Psychologist* in November 1984 documenting some psychologists' early research on HIV prevention. In his introduction he used the argument that only behavioral responses could halt the epidemic and critiqued the lack of funding allocated to the NIMH. Gay and bisexual men's perspectives were missing from biomedical research where 'a pervasive ignorance of gay life and gay sex has made much of the research designs, and consequent findings, questionable.'[13] Thomas Coates' research group in San Francisco was the only one represented here to report NIMH funding. Drawing on the emerging field of 'psychoneuroimmunology' they raised questions about the effects of an AIDS diagnosis on *stress*, and described the virus as a necessary but not a sufficient cause of AIDS. They argued for investigation of factors, other than sexual behaviors, that might make immunocompromise and infection more likely.[14] Writing from Columbia University in New York, John Martin and Carole Vance argued against the dominance of the 'germ theory' in favor of an interactive model that included 'lifestyle factors' in its explanation of AIDS diseases.[15] All researchers recognized the importance of *engaged* methods and active listening to gay and bisexual men such that research questions were informed by their concerns. Jill Joseph and her colleagues described at length the steps that they had taken to garner the trust necessary to construct research questions that would be relevant to gay and bisexual men.[16] With his colleagues, Stephen Morin, who was now counseling gay men with AIDS in San Francisco, sketched the psychological impact on men confronting uncertainty and certainty about death. Morin also interviewed Mervyn Silverman, the Director of Health in San Francisco who described that city's holistic response to the crisis.[17] A short article by Anthony Ferrara, who was living with AIDS, further demonstrated the psychologists' commitment to giving voice to gay men who were directly affected. Linking stigma to matters of life and death, Ferrara's article poignantly ended 'We are not bad people. We are merely gay, and that is no reason to regard us with disdain. Those of us physically unable to carry on this message look to you for champions.'[18] Ferrara died before the Special Feature went to print. The holistic nature of this early response, including humanistic counseling and engagement with political officials, is hard to square with critiques of lesbian and gay psychologists in this period as mere individualists who fail to challenge the status quo.

The emphasis on doing better science by drawing on the experience of the people whom that science represented, such as Ferrara, was also far from orthodox in the APA in the early 1980s. By 1981, as the first reports of KS appeared, two distinct groups of psychologists had claimed representation of lesbian and gay concerns within the APA. The Task Force on the States of Lesbian and Gay Male Psychologists continued its work into the late 1970s, and in 1980, the APA Council of Representatives created the Committee on Gay Concerns as an ongoing structure within BSERP. Independently, in 1977 Harvard graduate student William Paul initiated a Task Force on Sexual Orientation within Division 9 of the APA: the Society for the Psychological Study of Social Issues (SPSSI). As Michael Pettit narrates, the two groups clashed briefly over the responsibility to represent lesbian and gay concerns in a way that highlighted tensions about speaking from experience as a basis for representing these concerns. Barbara Sang of the BSERP group wrote to APA President Lawrence Wrightsman objecting that the SPSSI group had voiced that its actions would be *more* valid for the inclusion of 'nongays' in the group. Sang insisted that the Task Force should include a majority of self-identified gay psychologists and take care to address gender and ethnic representation. Wrightsman replied that researchers' sexuality was irrelevant, but rather that *sympathetic* attitudes were the key.[19]

After 1984 both scientists and the public quickly came to understand HIV as the necessary cause of AIDS, and all other lifestyle factors as facilitating causes. Controversially, local politicians ordered the closure of bathhouses in San Francisco and New York in 1984 and 1985 where men went for sex.[20] In 1985, the CDC definition of AIDS changed to include the new virus, blood banks began screening blood supplies, and the first commercial 'AIDS test' was licenced. In 1986 the USA and France agreed to share credit for the discovery of the virus, and the profits from sales of the ELISA test.[21] Developments in biomedical science had complex effects on the life chances of people living with AIDS and the psychological issues that they faced. AIDS tests made the *privacy* of HIV-positive (HIV+) people a point of political tension. In a move that was calculated to be controversial, leading conservative author William F. Buckley opined in March 1985 that 'everyone detected with AIDS should be tattooed in the upper forearm, to protect common needle-users, and on the buttocks, to protect the victimization of other homosexuals.' Buckley's views were not unique: opinion polls in 1985 and 1986 found that over 50% of respondents favored some sort of governmental regulation of sexual activity, and more had avoided public restrooms and homosexual people than had started to use condoms as a personal response to AIDS.[22] For many who considered themselves HIV-negative, the response to the epidemic was to try to draw a *cordon sanitaire* around it to protect 'the public,' often forgetting, sometimes deliberately, that people with AIDS and affected communities were also part of that same public.

The identification of a group of HIV+ people also prompted drug therapies that targeted the virus' mechanisms; several were introduced at the first International AIDS Conference in 1985.[23] As large sections of the gay public remained sceptical of medical authority, and some publications with large gay readerships voiced and amplified that scepticism, the relationship between 'treatment' and 'experimentation' remained blurred. In September 1986, a Phase II human trial of Burroughs-Wellcome's treatment AZT was suspended. Although the trial had not run to completion, the data so strongly suggested that AZT was effective that it was deemed unethical to continue to deny it to the control group. This decision exemplifies the conflict of interest between the immediate needs of HIV+ people for effective treatment, and existing standards for demonstrating that new drugs were safe. In 1987, the FDA approved AZT, without completing the Phase III

trial. By the FDA's established research norms, in place since the release of tha-
lidomide in the early 1960s, the drug was neither categorically safe nor categorically unsafe, and its presence heightened an 'epidemic of signification' about the
causes and nature of HIV.[24]

Increasingly, people with AIDS became involved in brokering expertise and
determining what science did and did not get done. In San Francisco, the new
publication *AIDS Treatment News* quickly became a trusted source of community-
based expertise on biomedical information. In New York the political group ACT
UP formed in response to Larry Kramer's (2005 [1983]) call to protest the
mismanagement, neglect, and lack of media attention to the epidemic through
direct action. In one key protest, ACT UP members shut down the Food and
Drug Administration.

The science and politics of HIV/AIDS were inseparable and urged responses
that often learned from postmodern challenges to the status of empirical science
as separable from politics. Such challenges increasingly drew on the insight that
language constructed the objects of science. Challenging scientific institutions and
authorities did not require the belief that science was meaningless or that good
science was not worth fighting for, and this attitude was best described by the
activist and cultural studies scholar Paula Treichler:

> Of course, where AIDS is concerned, science can usefully perform its inter-
> pretive part: we can learn to live – indeed, *must* learn to live – as though
> there are such things as viruses. The virus – a constructed scientific object – is
> also a historical subject, a 'human immunodeficiency virus,' a real source of
> illness and death that can be passed from one person to another under certain
> conditions that we can apparently – individually and collectively – influence.
> The trick is to live with this disjuncture, but the lesson is imperative.[25]

Between 1986 and 1988, the failures of an exclusively biomedical response to
HIV/AIDS became more obvious in the halls of power. The 1986 National
Academy of Sciences report *Confronting AIDS* could report little progress in the
behavioral or social sciences, but noted, again, the lack of funding. In 1987,
Surgeon General Everett Koop issued a report responding to the widespread
public misunderstanding about HIV transmission and took the unprecedented step
of mailing an information leaflet on prevention to every home in the United
States.[26] Koop broadcast and nationalized a version of the safer sex advice that
had originated in Callen and Berkowitz's pamphlet. People with AIDS also found
surprising allies in President Reagan's Commission on AIDS, which first met in
1987 and published its final report in 1988. Despite its many conservative
appointees, the Commission ultimately issued reports calling for a $20 billion ten-
year effort to fight AIDS and supported anti-discrimination laws protecting
people with AIDS.[27]

This national recognition that HIV/AIDS was a social and behavioral issue as
well as a biomedical one created a more fertile environment for psychologists to
play a part in responding to HIV/AIDS. In 1987, a stream of panels on

'Psychology and AIDS' ran through the 1987 APA convention, and in 1988, Bachelor achieved a new grant from NIMH for a training contract for psychologists. The APA had come to occupy a strategic position in lobbying for increased funding for behavioral research and mental health provision in response to AIDS. These activities broke with the model established early in Reagan's presidency to deprioritize the funding of social research.[28] The opening up of opportunities for psychological research in response to AIDS galvanized a larger number of psychologists to invest in behavior change and mental health interventions. In the 1988 convention, over fifty panels addressed AIDS, and several papers were developed and published in *American Psychologist* in November 1988, organized into five sections: *Overview, Primary Issues, Scientific Issues, Clinical and Counseling Issues,* and *Education and Prevention: Special Issues, and Organizational Issues*. It is harder to see where the contours of concern and opportunism meet in this response by psychologists than it is to detect a shift to make gay and bisexual men more normative populations of concern than before. Research on prevention of HIV/AIDS among gay and bisexual men fell in the 'Primary Issues' section, whilst reports on similar research on ethnic minority women, children and adolescents, and haemophiliacs made up the 'Education and Prevention: Special Issues' section.

The overview framed the federal and financial issues by demonstrating a new agreement to prioritize behavioral research on HIV/AIDS through NIMH. Admiral Watkins described the lack of behavioral research as inhibiting his Presidential Commission in reaching its findings.[29] In the 'Primary Issues' section, Morin described the holistic San Francisco model, as giving 'public health officials new hope that prevention efforts designed to facilitate behavior change can control the spread of HIV.' The epidemic was a threefold problem of AIDS diseases, HIV transmission, and 'the social, cultural, economic, and political reaction to the HIV and AIDS epidemics.'[30] Stall and his San Francisco colleagues described how 'dramatic changes have occurred' in gay and bisexual men's practices of unprotected anal sex, 'the amount and kinds of which probably exceed anything documented to date in the public health literature.'[31] This rapid behavior change seemed to be good news for health psychologists: gay and bisexual men exemplified the rapid changes in health-related behavior that health psychology promised it could bring about. However, a closer reading of these articles shows that gay and bisexual men changed their sexual practices before any health psychologists implemented any systematic behavior change programs. Des Jarlais similarly described how IV drug users in New York had changed their practices in response to concerns about HIV long before any governmental behavior change programs targeting them were implemented.[32]

Herek and Glunt's (1988) piece on AIDS stigma was also positioned to address a primary issue: social psychology was central to psychologists' responses to HIV/AIDS. Herek and Glunt eschewed the terms 'AIDS-phobia' and 'AIDS hysteria' in favor of *AIDS stigma*, consistent with Herek's preference for 'heterosexism' over 'homophobia.' AIDS stigma was worsened by fears about illness and the prejudices attached to marginalized groups associated with AIDS; primarily gay and bisexual men, but also IV drug users and ethnic minorities. Drawing further on

Herek's theory about the functions of heterosexist attitudes, Herek and Glunt argued that AIDS stigma had multiple causes, and that AIDS education had to engage with the stigmatization of groups associated with HIV/AIDS if it was to be effective. Any effective psychological response to HIV/AIDS had to be gay-affirmative.

By 1988, the disproportionate effect of the epidemic on ethnic minority Americans, particularly on African-Americans, was evident to psychologists. Peterson and Marín noted that emerging models of behavioral prevention in psychology would not address Black and Hispanic men who had sex with men if those interventions remained insensitive to culture. Most obviously, Black and Hispanic men were less likely than Whites to identify as 'gay' and so less likely to see themselves represented in education programs.[33] Ethnic minority women were even more over-represented within CDC statistics than their male counterparts. Susan Cochran and Vickie Mays presented a deep analysis of how and why prevention efforts 'consistent with the cultural norms and politics developed within the gay liberation movement,' would likely fail Black and Hispanic/Latina women affected by poverty. Their target was the kind of broadcast messages that were informed by norms such as 'safer sex.' Poorer ethnic minority women might not share the values that informed these interventions; they might not conceptualize sex as 'play' for religious reasons, they might be obliged to remain ignorant of sex until marriage, they might rely on sex as employment, and they might not disclose a HIV+ status to a potential partner because 'the risk of being alone and unsuccessful in relationships may seem greater than the risk of having transmitted AIDS.'[34]

By 1988, there had been little coverage of HIV/AIDS among African-Americans in popular media aimed at any audience.[35] African-Americans were not only over-represented among HIV+ people, but under-represented in clinical trials, and later reports suggested that African-Americans responded worse to AZT than other groups. Such findings and the activists that insisted on their relevance prompted the 1993 NIH Revitalization Act which required funded research to include representative samples of women and ethnic minorities.[36]

The section on social psychology particularly shows variability in the importance placed on context. Health psychologist Jeffrey Fisher described the ad hoc category of 'AIDS-preventive behaviors' (APBs) that shared only the features that they prevented HIV transmission, and that their uptake could be affected by social norms targeted by health promotion. Gay men more comfortable with being gay were more involved in networks that supported APBs, and affirmed the importance of gay identity for health in ways that would have seemed very marginal a decade earlier. However, like the identity models described in the last chapter, such thinking about identity could be normalizing, and could risk creating the very kind of racial and ethnic inequalities *among* gay and bisexual men described by Peterson and Marín.

A second way forward was to return to Kinsey-style surveys of sexual behavior. Kinsey Institute researchers drew together findings from Kinsey's studies and later sex surveys, to argue for the merits of Kinsey's original research methods and for larger funded studies of sexual behavior (conducted by experienced and independent researchers such as themselves).[37] The HIV epidemic required a knowledge of how people had sex, and particularly how men had sex with each other, and the traditional psychiatric paradigm was of absolutely no utility in preparing for this epidemic. The sex survey genre had languished since Kinsey's studies had had their funding cut short for political reasons. Whilst Kinsey's studies had focused on sexual behavior and not on identity group, in the 1970s the National Gay Task Force, anxious to construct a proportion of the population as gay/lesbian, had re-interpreted the Kinsey data by categorizing those participants who scored above an arbitrary cut-off on the scale as homosexual, and those below as heterosexual. The result was the mythic statistic that 10% of the population were gay/lesbian, which took hold as an assumption in AIDS epidemiology because there were no plausible alternatives to it.[38] The reinterpretation was significant and widespread. Kinsey did not use 0–6 scales in his interviews, and abandoned questionnaire-based methods very early on in his research program.[39] In the early 1990s, the first national attempt to quantify the sexual behavior of the United States since Kinsey was funded, in response to the lack of data that might inform national behavioral prevention responses to HIV/AIDS.[40] The resulting figures were challenging for lesbian and gay organizations, as they suggested that far less than 10% of the population had more than incidental histories of homosexual activity.[41]

The contributions of biological psychologists to the special issue were fewer and far less relevant to the concerns of people affected by HIV/AIDS. An article on virology ventured little that was *psychological*, beyond claiming that depression and lethargy induced by HIV might affect compliance with medical treatments.[42] A review of psychoneuroimmunology concluded that 'the study of immunity and stress in the HIV-positive, ARC, or AIDS patient can provide important information about the nature of the stress-immunity relation as well as about the disease itself.'[43] Somewhat more sympathetically, Kiecolt-Glaser and Glaser's review of psychological influences on immunity concluded that whilst HIV+ people experienced considerable stress, and particularly needed social support to buffer it, 'the simple presumption that an individual is in a high-risk group can produce considerable animosity.'[44] As this privileging of pure science over the needs of those who were living precariously with AIDS suggests, biological psychologists' investment in value-free science only appears to avoid important matters of value, ethics, and politics that HIV made inescapable. As Treichler would have it, science could play its interpretive part, but was not a discourse free of signification or of *partial* interest in people with HIV.

In sum, by 1988, HIV/AIDS structured opportunities for a very diverse range of psychologists and sexologists to engage existing, developing, and long-neglected forms of research to address a national priority. By so doing, they moved gay and bisexual men's health into a more normative position. Funding in HIV provided reasons to be 'gay affirmative' to many more psychologists beyond the marginal area of lesbian, gay, and bisexual psychology. Indeed, it became possible to articulate – as Cochran and Mays did – that gay culture had become *too* normative in the national response to HIV/AIDS.

In the late 1980s and afterwards, the narrative of exemplary behavior change among gay and bisexual men began to shift. Men who had sex with other men would often struggle to conform to – or struggle deliberately against – health psychologists' high hopes for conformity to health-producing norms in their daily sex lives. Practices such as 'negotiated safety' developed to manage sex lives that included both long-term lovers and casual partners, and researchers have since then continued to debate the extent to which norms in gay culture are affected by the health advice of earlier years that was designed to shape them. From the mid-1980s until the development of Highly Active Antiretroviral Therapy (HAART), HIV/AIDS research yielded rich studies of sexual practices in many diverse communities, often distinguishing sexual *practices* embedded in and formed by local contexts of meaning from 'behaviors' which can be counted and quantified with less regard to contexts. After the emergence of HAART rapidly increased life expectancy for HIV+ people in the mid-1990s, men began to engage in 'strategic positioning' to carve out different practices to manage risk, pleasure, safety, and intimacy.[45]

The Committee on Lesbian and Gay Concerns and the emergence of Division 44

Of course, HIV personally affected the experiences of psychologists who organized to represent lesbian and gay concerns *within* the APA in the 1980s also. As social psychologist Gregory Herek recalled from the mid-1990s:

> The toll on our profession also has been substantial. As far as I know, no formal tally exists of the number of psychologists, sociologists, psychiatrists and others who have died from AIDS. Even informal counts, however, are staggering. I find now that my time at annual conventions of the APA and other professional associations inevitably includes moments of reverie about my colleagues and friends who are not in attendance – because they are dead or too ill to travel – or for whom this may be the last meeting.[46]

Upon its formation as a permanent committee within BSERP in 1980, the Committee on Gay Concerns continued to keep track of affirmative research, and affirmative psychologists, and wrote pamphlets and teaching materials to challenge stereotypes with facts. In 1981, a Task Force began to develop a proposal for a Division of the APA, which was accepted in August 1984, creating Division 44 from January 1985 onwards. It elected fellows and officers, distributed achievement awards, encouraged mentoring, and aimed to be a 'home' for its members, 'a kind of family, a source of peer support, and a resource that has been difficult to find in a heterosexist society.'[47]

As Barbara Sang's letter to Lawrence Wrightsman shows, concerns with the presentation of diverse experience also characterized lesbian and gay groups in the APA from the outset, and butted up against empiricist norms that the value of psychological science was independent of the identity of the person who carried it out. Division 44 embedded principles of gender and ethnic minority representation in both its committee structures and its awards at a time when such principles were far from typical in American psychology. In 1997, Division 44 published a book-length catalog of the abstracts of the psychological and behavioral literature on gay and lesbian issues from 1985–1996. The list of categories had extended beyond Morin's five to an eighteen-page index. The most frequently addressed topic, by far, was *homosexuality (attitudes toward)*. The next most commonly addressed topics included *heterosexuality, bisexuality, psychosexual behavior*, and *psychosexual development*. Whether we were gay, lesbian, bi, or straight, whether our identities and behaviors lined up neatly or not, 'lesbian and gay issues' were about all of us by now, and the concern that most commonly unified those issues was *prejudice*.[48]

Prejudice was also being given more gravitas within various branches of the government beyond HIV/AIDS. Lesbian and gay community organizations had, by the late 1980s, managed to gain national recognition of the reality of heterosexist prejudice and the harms that it caused in everyday life. From 1984, the National Lesbian and Gay Task Force (NLGTF) and other community groups conducted surveys attesting to the frequency of anti-gay hate crimes, adding to a growing sense that anti-lesbian/gay violence was rising, fueled in part by fears about AIDS. In 1987 a Department of Justice report described hate crimes perpetrated on the basis of sexual orientation as surprisingly prevalent and especially violent. The 1990 Hate Crimes Statistics Act required the Department of Justice to collect and publish annual national hate crime statistics based on race, religion, sexuality, and ethnicity.[49]

Such developments created new conditions for the expansion of lesbian and gay psychology research. Brokering his own hypothesis that expressions of heterosexism have symbolic functions, Herek ventured that young heterosexual men might commit homophobic attacks as an externalization of gender conflicts and cause mental health damage as a result.[50] Herek and his colleagues completed original multi-method community surveys of LGB victims of hate crimes in Northern California. Many lesbians reported more sexual assaults, but most other kinds of hate crime were reported most often by gay men. Attacks were often committed by groups of strangers close to gay venues, but some had occurred in victims' homes. Symptoms of anxiety, depression, and posttraumatic stress disorder (PTSD) were more common among LGB people victimized by hate crimes, and these symptoms often led victims to withdraw from public life and were much more clearly evident among lesbians and gay men than among bisexual women and men.[51] In NLGTF surveys in the 1980s lesbians and gay men commonly reported that hate crimes were enacted on them *by* the police. Gay and lesbian respondents also described to Herek and his colleagues a decade later how they had not reported crimes out of fear of the police and fear of exposure of their sexual orientations.[52] In 1998, the vicious murder of 21-year-old college student Matthew Sheperd in Laramie, Wyoming brought such hate crimes to national attention, but their causes and consequences had been researched by psychologists extensively in the preceding decade.

The effects of heterosexism on the mental health of LGB young people also became increasingly recognized. Psychiatrist Emery Hetrick and his partner

Damien Martin formed the 'Institute for the Protection of Lesbian and Gay Youth,' later the Harvey Milk School in New York City in 1979.[53] In 1988, the National Education Association resolved that all students should have equal educational opportunities, regardless of sexual orientation. A year later the US Department of Health and Human Services published a controversial report noting that gay youth were two–three times more likely to attempt suicide than their heterosexual counterparts.[54] Psychologists' studies of the largely Hispanic and Black young people attending Hetrick-Martin revealed that suicide attempts were common, and that distress was related to unwanted life events whether gay-related or not.[55] Anthony D'Augelli and his colleagues worked with multiple organizations to scope the increased suicide risk among young LGB people, concluding that young people who had lost friends after coming out were most at risk.[56] Several studies confirmed increased suicide risk over the 1990s.[57] By the end of the decade, the organization Gay Lesbian and Straight Education Network had begun to publish annual reports of the national school climate and the measures taken to improve it.

The emerging views of the COGC (after 1985, the Committee on Lesbian and Gay Concerns, COLGC) were reported in a special feature of *American Psychologist* in 1991. In its introduction, Stephen Morin and Esther Rothblum, honored that year by Division 44 for her Distinguished Scientific Contribution, described '15 years of progress' since the APA's initial 1975 resolution on homosexuality. The relationship between the social sciences and the lesbian and gay civil rights movement was described as a close one, anchored by Kinsey's and Hooker's research and continuing in recent debates about *ego-dystonic homosexuality*, new trends in affirmative psychotherapy, the recognition of lesbians and gay men in hate crimes statistics, and the exclusion of same-gender sexual orientation from the Americans with Disabilities Act. Strikingly, no reference at all was made to HIV/AIDS or its relationship to lesbian and gay psychology's struggles, achievements, and contemporary challenges.[58]

Feminist psychologists thinking about language and implicit identity norms clearly influenced several papers in this volume. Morin and Rothblum cited recent research by Janet Hyde on *masculine generics* that took men to be the norm.[59] By 1991, psychologists were no longer using such language in their research writing.[60] In the early 1980s, feminist psychologists had also theorized that women and men view the world differently, and that psychology had overlooked women's distinct ways of knowing.[61] Yet, the question of what constituted 'fact' and what constituted 'stereotype' in these debates remained difficult; some feminists voiced justified worries that claims about gender difference could be used as a hook for patriarchy as readily as the denial of difference.[62] Feminist debates about describing empirical sex differences and similarities often touched on *androcentrism*, theorized by Sandra Bem as a dynamic that took men to be the norm, located difference in women, and worked to women's structural disadvantage.[63] Some feminist psychologists were influenced by postmodernist thinking which opened up questions about what different descriptions of gender similarities and differences *do*.[64] Such thinking about assumed identity norms was particularly transferable to *heterosexism*; AIDS among gay men had been prematurely assumed to be the 'effect' that epidemiologists needed to explain, gay men were considered to be a group that 'the public' needed to be protected from in the context of HIV/AIDS, bisexual men were imagined to be a group that might transmit HIV to the 'normal population,' and lesbians and bisexual women were tainted with courtesy stigma, particularly when they aligned themselves with AIDS work.

The Special Feature of 1991 shows lesbian and gay psychologists actively joining this conversation about how methods, concepts, and language construct realities. The short report on 'Avoiding Heterosexist Bias in Language' described implicit effects of language on the meaning of group identity, recommending *gay men* and *lesbians* over *homosexuals* as the former represent 'modern culture and communities' rather than sickness (or representing only men). Anticipating more recent calls for less cisgenderist and bi-inclusive language, the phrase *opposite sex* was criticized as polarizing, and researchers were urged 'to avoid the erroneous impression that all people relate exclusively to one gender.'[65] Herek and his colleagues' Guidelines for Conducting Non-Heterosexist Research extended these concerns to address substantive methodological decisions that researchers might make. They warned against asking questions that presumed that lesbians, gay men, and bisexuals did not exist, or asking questions in ways that presumed stereotypes were true, or asking questions that assumed LGB people were necessarily less healthy or normal that heterosexual people, or asking questions that merely singled LGB people out as the explanation of group difference:

> For example, research on the development of *sexual orientation* (which treats heterosexuality, bisexuality, and homosexuality as equally requiring of explanation) has the potential of improving scientific understanding of human sexuality. In contrast, research is unlikely to yield only scientifically important findings if it seeks cause only for homosexuality and omits heterosexuality from the investigation.[66]

Herek et al. understood that the solution to othering was not to either 'turn the volume up' or 'turn the volume down' but to undo the habits of describing LGB people primarily in terms of their *deviation* from norms that heterosexual people were presumed to occupy. Similarly, the COLGC recommendations on language urged authors to increase the visibility of lesbians, gay men, and bisexuals in contexts unrelated to sexual behavior, and to compare lesbians and gay men with actual heterosexual people rather than 'the general public.' Here, The COLGC's work anticipated Bem's point that lower-status groups quickly became 'the effect to be explained' when differences were described.

There were ontological and epistemological tensions within these papers that mirrored broader cross-disciplinary debates about essentialism and constructionism in gay, lesbian, and queer studies, discussed in the next chapter. The guidelines' insistence that psychologists think and write as if gay men, lesbians, and bisexuals exist was in tension with the recognition of Herek and his colleagues that 'homosexuality' is a cultural construction that does not apply in all cultures and historical periods. The preference for language terms that reflected the views of modern lesbian and gay communities assumed that preferences for language terms were homogeneous in those communities, quite in contrast to assertions elsewhere that lesbians, gay men, and bisexuals shared *nothing* in common beyond their sexual orientation. As feminist psychologists pointed out, challenging one set of normative identities, such as heterosexuality, often did little more than re-inscribing new norms for identity.[67] But in calling attention to these tensions, my intention is not to reveal or denigrate 'bias,' but to notice the problems that are made visible when a marginalized group goes beyond critiquing the 'bias' to which they have been subject and begins the more difficult task of articulating new ideals with which all can identify. Moreover Division 44's commitment to representing intersections of sexuality with race and gender was not inevitable, and was certainly not shared by parallel organizations, in psychiatry, for example. Herek's advice on research was a set of 'guidelines,' a term that the APA increasingly used to describe ideals, in contrast to 'standards' which should be followed in all circumstances. They held out the promise of what exceptional researchers might do if they broke with the unthinking norms of representing lesbians, gay men, and bisexuals only as oddities, natural experiments, or as people whose lives could be assumed to be damaged and limited.

By its very logic, empirical psychology creates particular difficulties for minority group projects that must debunk stereotypes about group differences. Psychological research then as now, tends to emphasize and amplify findings of group differences more than findings of group similarities. The ideals expressed in the new guidelines speak to the twin threats of invisibility and spectacle with which LGB people are faced. Lesbian and gay psychologists could most easily avoid these problems by continuing to reverse the gaze away from the nature of group differences with an emphasis on prejudice. Fewer lesbian and gay psychologists than feminists engaged explicitly with the postmodernist challenges to the very rationale for science.[68] Rather, engaging the state through the courts took priority over such intellectual questions.

In sum, by the late 1980s the need to articulate a gay-affirmative perspective, particularly by asserting the importance of *heterosexism*, became more evident as pollsters, community groups, and government departments all caught up with the recognition that *heterosexism* or *homophobia* was a real thing. Whilst psychological research in this area continued to be marginal and to represent a very small percentage of all psychological research in the 1990s, the equation of heterosexism with sexism and racism appeared more legitimate than a decade earlier. In the 1990s, Division 44 published an annual book series, awarded research grants and prizes, including the Wayne Placek Awards given to honor one of the research participants in Hooker's original study.

In the 1990s, psychologists' claims on 'sexuality' were challenged on the one hand by biologists and psychiatrists, for whom *heterosexism* was not a central organizing principle. Elsewhere in the social sciences and humanities, lesbian, gay, and queer studies opened up new challenges to all forms of scientific knowledge about sexuality by engaging with postmodernism and poststructuralism to a far greater extent than the 'liberal humanist' psychologists would do. Of course, the boundaries of disciplines sometimes blurred. Most obviously, the new journal *Feminism & Psychology* under the editorship of Sue Wilkinson, became a new, international venue for research, debate, and historiography that published on such matters as heterosexuality, the politics of therapy for lesbians, and the value (if any) of sex differences research for feminism.[69] *Feminism & Psychology* not only foregrounded social constructionism, it did not take the USA as its normative context – the first venue for lesbian and gay psychology that did not do so. At the same time, the APA was also challenged by the formation of the Association for Psychological Science, a new organization with far less commitment to humanism and egalitarianism as organizing principles of psychology.[70] Psychology was diversifying once again. Which would be the best ontological, epistemological, ethical, and political understanding of 'sexuality'? Increasingly, the important answers to this question were decided in court.

Notes

1 Martin (1994).
2 Van Voorhis & Wagner (2002).
3 See Berridge (2011), Fee & Fox (1988).
4 Silvestre (2008).
5 Harvey (1990).
6 Henriques et al. (1984).
7 Pickren & Schneider (2005).
8 Here, and for much of the history of AIDS science, I rely primarily on Epstein (1996).
9 Fisher (1983).
10 Cohen (1997a).
11 Berkowitz & Callen (1997 [1983]), Callen & Berkowitz (1997 [1982]).
12 Kimmel & Browning (1999, p. 145); Matarazzo et al. (1988, pp. 978–979).
13 Bachelor (1984, p. 1281).
14 Coates, Temoshok & Mandel (1984).
15 Martin & Vance (1984).
16 Joseph et al. (1984).
17 Morin, Charles, & Maylon (1984); Morin (1984).
18 Ferrara (1984, p. 1287).
19 Pettit (2011).
20 For a detailed journalistic history of these events see Shilts (1987). For an insightful critique of Shilts see Crimp (1987).
21 Epstein (1996).
22 Buckley (1986), Singer, Rogers, & Corcoran (1987, pp. 592, 594).
23 Epstein (1996).
24 Treichler (1987).
25 Treichler (1987, p. 69).
26 Koop (1986).
27 Presidential Commission (1988).
28 Matarazzo et al. (1988).
29 Watkins (1988).
30 Morin (1988, p. 838).
31 Stall, Coates, & Hoff (1988, p. 878).
32 Des Jarlais & Friedman (1988).

33 Peterson and Marín (1988).
34 Mays and Cochran (1988, pp. 954).
35 Cohen (1997a).
36 Epstein (2007).
37 Reinisch et al. (1988).
38 Voeller et al. (1990).
39 Hegarty (2013).
40 Laumann et al. (1994).
41 Accordingly from the mid-1990s onward, gay and lesbian organizations often cited the 10% Kinsey figure whilst more homophobic organizations cited the lower figure that emerged from the NORC survey. See Pruitt (2002).
42 Hall (1988, p. 912).
43 Baum & Nesselhoff (1988, p. 903).
44 Kiecolt-Glaser & Glaser (1988, p. 896).
45 Kippax & Race (2003).
46 Herek (1995, p. ix).
47 Kimmel & Browning (1999, pp. 133–137).
48 Anderson & Adley (1997). This collection also exemplifies the construction of lesbian and gay psychology as a field that is *not* about HIV/AIDS, indeed to contain the literature review to a manageable size the authors excluded literature that also referenced AIDS and HIV (p. 226).
49 See Berrill (1989), Herek (1989), Herek & Berrill (1992).
50 Garnets, Herek, & Levy (1992), Herek (1989).
51 Herek, Gillis, & Cogan (1999, pp. 948–949).
52 Herek, Cogan, & Gillis (2002), Herek, Gillis, & Cogan (1999).
53 See Hunter (2007).
54 Maher et al. (2009).
55 See Rosario, Rotheram-Borus, & Reid (1996), Rotheram-Borus, Hunter, & Rosario (1994).
56 Hershberger, Pilkington, & D'Augelli (1997). See also D'Augelli & Hershberger (1993), Hirschberger & D'Augelli (1995).
57 Savin-Williams and Ream (2003).
58 Morin & Rothblum (1991).
59 Hyde (1984).
60 Gannon et al. (1992).
61 See Belenky et al. (1986); Gilligan (1982).
62 For a criticism of Gilligan's claims about gender differences in moral reasoning see Greeno & Maccoby (1986). For an early insightful essay on how feminism grounded in psychological differences might be used to justify sexism see Mednick (1989).
63 Bem (1993).
64 See particularly the essays in Hare-Mustin & Marecek (1990).
65 Committee on Lesbian and Gay Concerns (1991).
66 Herek et al. (1991, p. 958).
67 Hegarty et al. (2013).
68 Hare-Mustin & Marecek (1990); Riger (1992); Wetherell (1997).
69 On heterosexuality see Kitzinger, Wilkinson, & Perkins (1992); on therapy see Perkins (1991) and on sex differences see Kitzinger (1994).
70 Cautin (2009).

4 Taking the case to court

In the last chapter, I examined how gay-affirmative perspectives built new forms of psychology upon the recognition of heterosexism as a social problem that affected mental and physical health. One of the surest historical effects of this process has been the ways in which the APA has engaged US law in cases where lesbians' and gay men's rights have been at stake. The APA has recently published online all of the amicus curiae briefs that it has submitted.[1] In spite of the vast range of issues that might be considered 'psychological' in recent American history, the APA has spoken to US law more often to affirm lesbian, gay, and bisexual citizens' rights than for any other potentially *psychological* issue at all. Amicus curiae briefs or 'amicus briefs' are often offered by professional associations that are not litigants in a case to establish in law matters that have become a consensus in their own fields. The APA legal briefs build on the new affirmative consensus developed in the 1970s, persistently argue that homosexuality is normal rather than pathological, and describe lesbians and gay men as subject to a long history of prejudicial treatment. An earlier generation of psychiatrically informed law that had presumed the pathology of homosexuality prompted this activity, which reached a peak between 2010 and 2015 in cases regarding equal marriage.

This chapter examines this history of engagement with the law. Contemporary opinions vary among LGBT psychologists about the impact of the APA's actions in taking these issues to court. The 2009 Report on Gender Identity and Gender Variance describes the amicus briefs as the kind of activity that could be effective in Transgender Psychology.[2] Hammack and Windell describe in detail the testimony offered by psychologists Gregory Herek, Anne Peplau, and Ilan Meyer in the 2010 *Perry v. Schwarzenegger* case, and its influence upon Judge Walker's pivotal ruling, which challenged the constitutionality of withholding marriage licenses from same-sex couples as 'illustrative of the use of psychological science for transformative ends.'[3] In his 2012 Presidential Address to Division 44, Mark Pope celebrated particularly the 2003 US Supreme Court decision in *Lawrence v. Texas*, which ruled that state sodomy laws were unconstitutional, and the 2010 US Court of Appeals *Perry v. Schwarzenegger* decision. Harking back to Evelyn Hooker's and Magnus Hirschfeld's aim to achieve justice through science, Pope understood these achievements as the rewards for a tradition of 'facting,' presenting truth in the face of societal stereotype.[4]

Hammack and Windell also criticized the APA's engagement with the law on three grounds. The APA strategy sought to expand the category of the 'normal' to include sexual minorities without challenging the idea of normality, it was disconnected from appeals to human rights, and it eschewed the historical nature of sexual orientation categories. The APA may have done a lot, but these authors suggest that it might have done more to overturn the terms of normality by appealing on the one hand to universal notions of human rights and on the other to historically specific lived experiences of sexual minority people. Diamond and Rosky have argued that one plank of the legal argument for gay and lesbian rights is no longer necessary: the idea that lesbians and gay men deserve rights because sexual orientation is an *immutable* trait.[5] Immutability was emphasized in recent marriage cases, but as Diamond and Rosky argue, arguments from immutability may not lead judges to rule one way or another, and those arguments fail to recognize a 'silent majority' of sexual minority people, including people with bisexual sexual histories, people who change their sexual identity label, and people who experience some choice about the gender of their partners. From the mid-1990s onward, Division 44 claimed to represent not only gay and lesbian, but also *bisexual* concerns, but psychologists have researched bisexual-identified women and men far less often than their lesbian- and gay-identified counterparts.[6] Might the emphasis on immutability have contributed to the erasure of bisexuality in psychology? Amicus briefs are performative statements, aimed at affecting the matters that the law assumes to be the case. They also must represent matters of wide consensus within the profession to be legitimate. I examine these authors' concerns about the amicus briefs by looking in a little bit more detail at differences in the matters that the APA and others presented to the court.

Before doing so, it is necessary to describe something of the very distinct legal framework of the USA. Lesbian and gay psychology requires us to particularize the indigenous psychology of the recent USA,[7] which increasingly encountered global, as well as national, frameworks over the period examined here.[8] The APA's amicus briefs responded to a particular understanding of rights enshrined in the 14th Amendment to the US Constitution. This Amendment, enacted in 1868 after the Civil War, was a response to slavery, and required states to provide all of their citizens with *equal protection* under the law. In other words, state law cannot create arbitrary groupings of people and then discriminate against them in the exercise of the law. Federal and state laws that do treat groups unequally must have a rational basis or must pursue a compelling state interest if they are to survive a legal challenge on an equal-protection basis. In 1938 in the case of *United States v. Carolene Products*, the US Supreme Court established that prejudice towards 'discrete and insular' minority groups should trigger particular legal scrutiny.[9] Laws targeting such groups were deemed particularly 'suspect' and such groups were deemed *suspect classes*. Race and national origin were determined to be suspect classes in the 1940s, and by the 1980s, when the APA began to weigh in on lesbian and gay rights cases, gender and illegitimacy had also achieved quasi-suspect status.[10] Questions about the immutability, stigmatization, and political disenfranchisement of these groups all played a role in determining the suspect class status of these groups.[11] The entanglement of American psychology, minority group rights, and equal protection has long roots. In the landmark 1954 *Brown v. Board of Education* decision, the racial segregation of American schools was recognized as a violation of equal protection by Supreme Court justices informed by a brief prepared in 1952 by social psychologists in the SPSSI on the harms caused by legally enforcing perceptions of Black children's inferiority.[12]

Sexual minorities face two intersecting threats from unequal law, and psychology can inform them both. These threats are the unchecked denial of privacy (most acutely in our homes, and particularly in regard to privacy over sexual practices), and social discrimination on the basis of group identities in public. Of course, the people made vulnerable by these two threats might differ to some extent: not everyone who has sex with someone of the same gender identifies as lesbian, gay, or bisexual and vice versa. An entire edifice of homophobic law had been put in place, often by appeal to the diagnosis of homosexuals as sexual psychopaths in earlier periods of the twentieth century. Much of the history that follows concerns shifting arguments for the claim that sexual minorities constitute a suspect class to protect against these threats.

Below, I focus first on the emergence of APA legal activism. In recent decades, not only did lesbian, gay, and bisexual psychology flourish, but 'sexuality' became an object in an increasing range of academic disciplines. Many developments in the new fields of lesbian, gay, and queer studies challenged the view that lesbians and gay men were best understood as a social identity group, or that 'sexuality' was best understood as something psychological, rather than something historical, biological, sociological, or textual. To examine whether the APA strategy was insufficiently critical, I consider what it tried to do, and what it achieved, in its own time with respect to challenges and alternatives presented by both more biological and more sociological disciplines. I look particularly at the contrasts between psychology, psychiatry, and biology in the case of Colorado Amendement 2 which was determined in the US Supreme Court as *Romer v. Evans* in 1996. I next consider the differences between psychology and sociology in regard to parenting cases from the mid-1990s onward. Finally, I examine how these events and the *Lawrence* ruling changed the rules of the game, and set the context for the APA's support for equal marriage law in the twenty-first century.

The APA goes to court

Hooker's NIMH Task Force Report on homosexuality was controversial in its time for its opposition to sodomy laws. But over the 1970s and early 1980s, most of the United States either repealed their sodomy laws or greatly softened their penalties.[13] The 1991 Special Feature of *American Psychologist* that I described at the end of the last chapter includes an article examining the APA's emerging legal strategy activism in support of lesbian and gay rights. By then, five amicus briefs had already been submitted, the first two pertaining to cases testing the constitutional status of state sodomy laws.[14] In *New York v. Uplinger* (1984), Uplinger was arrested for soliciting sex from an undercover policeman, and – at the request of the Lamdba Legal Defense Fund who represented him – the APA submitted an amicus brief. The brief argued for the naturalness of the homosexual acts that the state sodomy law had criminalized, and cited research findings from the Kinsey studies onwards that attested to their ordinariness in homosexual and heterosexual contexts.[15] The US Supreme Court evaded the constitutional issues raised by the challenge to New York's sodomy law.

Unlike *Uplinger*, the case of *Bowers v. Hardwick* in the state of Georgia involved two men who had sex in private, and who were interrupted when a police officer entered Michael Hardwick's home to investigate a defunct warrant for Hardwick's arrest related to an earlier minor offense. Angered by his arrest in his own home, Hardwick sued the state's attorney general, Michael Bowers, and his case was supported by the American Civil Liberties Union (ACLU). The APA filed a joint amicus brief with the American Public Health Association (APHA) that upped the ante from the *Uplinger* brief by emphasizing not only that the sexual acts involved were not 'deviant,' but also that prohibiting them caused harm to many people – of diverse orientations – for whom they are essential for the expression and enactment of intimate relationships.[16] The brief also argued that Georgia's sodomy law undermined public health efforts against HIV/AIDS, because its penalties would lead gay people to closet themselves in their interactions with health professionals, and would impede attempts to teach about safer sex.[17] These arguments for allowing individuals to have privacy about their sexual conduct were mirrored in the 1988 special issue of *American Psychologist* on HIV/AIDS.[18] There, Herek and Glunt described state sodomy laws as creating 'an untenable situation in which safe-sex educational programs necessarily encourage criminal conduct; such laws should be overturned as part of an effective response to AIDS.'[19] Debating the merits of contact tracing to determine the epidemiology of HIV infection, Coates et al. also noted that, 'half of the states describe sodomy as a crime (and the U.S. Supreme Court has upheld the rights of the states to enact these laws).' Accordingly, if asked to supply the names of previous sexual contacts, 'those groups most likely to benefit from contact tracing will avail themselves of the opportunity to incriminate their friends and lovers.'[20]

In a historic, much criticized and now overturned judgment, five of the nine US Supreme Court justices upheld the Georgia sodomy statute in *Bowers*. Critically, understandings of the history of *heterosexism* informed their judgment. The justices described a long history of sodomy laws prohibiting homosexual sodomy with 'ancient roots' that are 'Firmly rooted in Judaeo-Christian moral and ethical standards.'[21] The minority of dissenting judges re-stated the point made by the APA-APHA brief that homosexuality was not disordered, and insisted that secular law required a justification beyond the expression of the morality of particular religious groups. Nonetheless, the majority judgment stood and Bowers cast a long shadow over lesbian and gay legal rights in the USA until its repeal in *Lawrence* in 2003.

It is significant that 'lesbian and gay psychology' as we came to know it, took shape in the particular national and legal context of the intervening years between *Bowers* and *Lawrence*. Beyond shifting attention to individual state laws in which the rights to engage in homosexual acts remained criminalized, *Bowers* was interpreted as limiting protection for lesbians and gay men against discrimination. In several decisions after *Bowers*, the 'conduct' of homosexuality was taken as defining a class of gay/lesbian people, and a class of people cannot claim protection on the basis of criminal conduct.[22] As in HIV/AIDS prevention and education efforts, with which sodomy laws were now intertwined, the question of the ontological relationship between being and acting gay/lesbian now became determinative. The situation of lesbians and gay men in the armed forces further pressed on this ontological question. During World War II, psychiatrists developed very specific codes that were informed by psychoanalytic theory for excluding psychiatric cases, including homosexuals, from the armed forces. Lesbians and gay men in the armed forces were vulnerable to exclusion unless they successfully closeted themselves.[23] In response to challenges from gay and lesbian people in the 1970s, in 1982 the US Department of Defense clarified its position that homosexuality was incompatible with military service.[24]

Miriam Ben-Shalom and Perry Watkins were both denied re-enlistment in the armed forces under this policy because they had been open about their sexual orientations, and the APA submitted amicus briefs in both of their cases.[25] Ben-Shalom argued that the army regulation infringed her right to free speech, and specifically to identify as a lesbian. She lost her case in the Seventh Circuit Court of Appeals, and the Supreme Court refused to review this decision. In contrast, Perry Watkins' case hung on the equal protection clause, as he claimed membership of a suspect class on the basis of his sexuality. His argument was supported by the long history of heterosexist treatment, its irrelevance to service in the armed forces, and the claim that sexual orientation is an immutable characteristic, like race.[26] The APA brief supported Watkins by prioritizing the claim that homosexuals are a 'discrete and insular minority' who had suffered discrimination throughout US history, that sexual orientation was highly resistant to change, that it had little impact on individuals' abilities to contribute to society, and that homosexuals were harmed by the military policy.[27] Watkins and his lawyers successfully argued that *Bowers* was not relevant to his case as it concerned *acts* and not *identities*. The appeals court ruled 2–1 in favor of Watkins' reinstatement, but avoided ruling on the constitutional challenge to the military policy raised by his case.

The military policy created long-standing tensions within the APA. In August 1991, the APA Council of Representatives publicly opposed the military policy by closing its publications to the US Department of Defense until its policy that homosexuality was incompatible with military service was rescinded.[28] In 1992, President Bill Clinton also campaigned on the promise to reverse the military policy, allowing lesbians and gay men to serve openly. In 1993 Gregory Herek spoke on behalf of the APA before the House Armed Services Committee, arguing that homosexuality was no bar to service, that concerns about homosexuals undermining troop cohesion were misplaced, and that the military should take a firm stand against anti-gay violence.[29] But Clinton encountered significant political opposition to his election promise and ultimately passed the notorious compromise of the 'don't ask, don't tell' (DADT) policy late in 1993. DADT protected closeted servicemen and women but allowed discharge of those who outed themselves through their speech or conduct, opening up closeted people in the armed forces to victimization and enormous ambiguity as to what constituted the speech act of coming out in a military context.[30] Far from creating equality, DADT incited curiosity: the more than 1,000 stories occasioned by this policy covered by TV networks rendered it the most frequently covered story about the Pentagon in the 1990s.[31]

Does biological immutability imply suspect class status?

In the *Watkins* and *Ben-Shalom* briefs, the APA argued that in regard to such matters as heterosexist treatment and immutability, 'the Court should take into account scientific research, much of it conducted by psychologists, and expert scientific issues concerning these very issues.'[32] American psychologists were not alone in claiming such authority over the epistemology of sexuality. In the post-*Bowers* context, legal advocates for lesbians, gay men, and bisexuals increasingly looked to suspect class status as a means of limiting the impact of *Bowers* on rights.

Psychiatrist Richard Green ventured the purest argument in favor of basing legal rights and claims on biological evidence of immutability.[33] His case was strengthened by the sudden emergence of several new biological studies of male sexuality. The most prominent of these were a behavioral genetics study by Michael Bailey and Richard Pillard, Simon LeVay's study of differences in the anterior hypothalamus of gay and straight men, and Dean Hamer and his colleagues' genetic linkage study, which found a difference on the X chromosome between gay and straight men, suggesting that male sexuality was inherited from one's mother.[34] All of these studies focused on men, tended to assume that sexual orientation was a binary variable (such that one was truly gay or straight in nature), and were largely produced by openly gay and ostensibly gay-affirmative authors. These authors were also warmly received in the USA by mainstream journalists, who presented the new biology as good news for lesbians and gay men as it showed that being homosexual was not one's own personal fault.[35]

The emergence of a *pro-gay* study of human biology was a turning point in the late 1980s and early 1990s. For example, in the 1970s German neuroscientist Gunter Dorner had argued that research linking sexual orientation and hormones should be used both to advise pregnant women how to prevent the birth of gay children and to change the sexual orientations of adults. Dorner's work drew on animal studies and on the historical evidence of increased rates of homosexuality among the men born in Germany in the years after World War II, attributed to hormonal deficiencies among deprived pregnant German women.[36] The view that homosexuality was a biologically based trait was at odds with lesbian and gay psychology's tradition of *disinterest* in questions about causality, examined in Chapter 2. However these biological studies fit better with a shift in *psychiatric* opinion in the early 1990s.

Lesbian and gay groups within the American Psychiatric Association were slower to gain recognition than their psychologist counterparts. The first meeting of the Association of Gay and Lesbian Psychiatrists (AGLP), led by Frank Rundle, occurred in 1978.[37] Gay and lesbian groups in psychiatry were also persistently male-dominated, in contrast to Division 44. The continuing diagnosis of homosexuality was also at odds with the organization of openly lesbian and gay psychiatrists who could be deemed to be categorically suffering from mental illness themselves. In the American Psychiatric Association's (1980) *DSM-III*, the diagnosis of Sexual Orientation Disturbance was replaced by Ego-Dystonic Homosexuality, and in *DSM-III-R* (1987), Ego-Dystonic Homosexuality was removed. Nonetheless, if you were motivated to do so, there remained loopholes in the diagnostic system by which homosexuality could be diagnosed.[38] In addition to protesting these rump diagnoses, the AGLP pushed the larger APA to make position statements on the psychiatric rationale for exclusion of lesbians and gay men from the military in 1984 and 1990, on discrimination (1988), and on dropping the definition of homosexuality as a mental illness by the Immigration and Naturalization Service in 1990.[39] In 1991, the APA issued a statement against discrimination against lesbians, gay men, and bisexuals in training for the profession, and in 1992, the organization issued a new position statement that called on organizations to work against the stigma that homosexuals had endured.[40] In other words, in the early 1990s, gay-affirmative perspectives were gaining ground in the American Psychiatric Association also.

The new biological studies appeared to demarcate gay-affirmative psychiatry from pseudoscience, particularly after a small group of psychiatrists formed a new organization, NARTH: the National Association for Research and Treatment of Homosexuality, which continued to apply psychiatry to 'cure' homosexuality. As psychiatrist Jack Drescher made clear, NARTH's position in the 1990s was opposed to affirmative perspectives in psychology, psychiatry, the social sciences, and the humanities. NARTH also increasingly took issue with the new genetic and neuroanatomy studies, as NARTH were deeply invested in claims that parent–child relationships were the cause of homosexuality, which – as such – warranted long-term psychotherapy.[41] In sum, in the early 1990s, American psychologists and psychiatrists differed in their reasons for rejecting the claim that sexual orientations were amenable to change, with some wishing to move away from suspicious questions about causality and others keen to answer them with the new biological findings.

Colorado Amendment 2 and the argument from immutability

The case of Colorado Amendment 2 tested the extent to which biological arguments were essential to progressive legal strategies.[42] By the early 1990s, Colorado had become the home of both visible queer communities, particularly in Denver, and of several 'Christian right' groups, who increasingly saw such communities as a primary target for activism, particularly in Colorado Springs. By 1991, several Colorado cities, including Denver, had enacted local anti-gay discrimination ordinances.[43] Ammendment 2 would have made such protections and all future protections on the basis of sexual orientation illegal within the state. Amendment 2 was one of very few cases that prompted an amicus brief from the American Psychiatric Association as well as from the American Psychological Association. Psychiatrists testified on both sides of the case;

both Richard Green and Richard Pillard argued the case for immutability. Charles Socarides, one of the NARTH's founders, argued against them.[44]

Amendment 2 was a voter initiative that aimed to render such ordinances illegal. Gay and lesbian advocates in the Amendment 2 case initially drew heavily on biological evidence to assert that sexual orientation was *immutable* to argue that lesbians and gay men constituted a suspect class, and that Amendment 2 deserved heightened scrutiny. But immutability is only one of several factors that inform the determination of a group as a 'suspect class.' A suspect class must also appear 'discrete and insular.' In the early 1990s, lesbian and gay lawyers often cited scientific studies to argue against the view that sexual orientation was chosen or mutable, although the question about immutability was rarely central to legal debates about lesbian and gay rights in this period.[45] But as Halley noted in regard to sexual minorities, 'anonymity and diffuseness produced by the closet are our chief organizing challenges, and they emerge from elements of our identity that are often radically mutable – public and private identity.'[46] Aware of the growing visibility and strength of bisexual and queer movements in the early 1990s that challenged essentialist 'lesbian and gay' models of identity politics, Halley noted that the argument from immutability was divisive within the very communities it was supposed to protect, a view that Diamond and Rosky echo. Indeed, the argument from immutability was tried and failed in 1993, in *Evans v. Romer*. The claim that sexual orientation was 'resistant to change' was heard as the claim that sexual orientation is inborn, and dismissed in court as unproven.[47]

Colorado Amendment 2 was ultimately adjudicated in the Supreme Court as *Romer v. Evans* (1996). In its amicus brief to the United States Supreme Court, the APA made its familiar arguments that homosexuality was normal and no impairment. The APA brief also cited the biological studies to refute the idea that sexuality is a choice. However, the APA brief adopted a not entirely consistent position on ontology, tempering citation of the biological studies with the claim that sexual orientations included bisexuality and were 'sometimes viewed as falling along a continuum.' This recognition of continua was timely, as Division 44 was also undergoing a shift towards representation of lesbian, gay *and bisexual* issues.[48] The distinction between sexual behavior and sexual identity was also emphasized and illustrated with research that heterosexuals sometimes engage in homosexual acts and lesbians and gay men sometimes engage in heterosexual acts. In sum, the 'silent majority' of sexual minority people with whom Diamond and Rosky are concerned were both recognized *and* erased in this brief.

These questions about the *nature* of sexual orientation were less determinative than questions about the nature of heterosexism. The APA brief described the history, nature, and effects of prejudice to conclude that Amendment 2 'rests on baseless stereotypes about gay people, and reflects the sort of historically rooted antipathy still common in our society.' In the Supreme Court, questions about the impact of prejudice were far more important than any of these questions about nature and nurture, or categories and continua. The Supreme Court judges recognized that *animus* lay behind the writing of Amendment 2 in the first place, shifting their gaze from questions about the nature of homosexuality to scrutinize and to name the motives of its authors. In a six–three ruling in May 1996, the justices deemed that Amendment 2 was 'invalid even on a modest reading of its implications' because it singled out a group of people for harm and aimed to deprive them of full political participation. Whether or not lesbians and gay men were a 'discrete and insular group' in reality, the judges recognized that Amendment 2 had targeted them as such. Lesbians and gay men were vulnerable to being disempowered unfairly, whether they were a discrete and insular group or not. This determination led to increased scrutiny of the claims that Amendment 2 promoted religious freedom, families' private rights to teach their children traditional moral values, or less specific arguments that heteronormativity was in the state interest. *Romer v. Evans* was the most significant victory in the courts for lesbian and gay advocates in the post-*Bowers* period.[49]

In reviewing this case, Cobb has insightfully noted different ways that *race* was used as an analogy for sexual orientation, both in court and in popular coverage. Whilst the case failed to compel the analogy that sexual orientation 'like race' is immutable, the judges' conclusions confirmed a different kind of analogy grounded in the vulnerability to being hated and singled out on the basis of *animus*. I would venture further that the case illustrates how heterosexism was shifting to become more modern, as racism had long since done. As Herman details, supporters of Colorado Amendment 2 developed the argument that lesbian and gay rights were not *equal* rights, but *special* rights. In his judgment, Justice Kennedy refuted this point about specialness: 'The protections that Amendment 2 denies to homosexuals have taken for granted [sic] by most people either because they already have them or do not need them.' When laws change and norms shift, prejudice can find a more modern expression in targeting activist groups who work for social equality as seeking 'special rights.' In the late 1990s, social psychologists began to theorize modern forms of heterosexism. The items on their attitude scales less often asked about beliefs about lesbians and gay men as groups, as on Herek's measures, and more often on opinions about initiatives such as gay pride parades, gay and lesbian studies classes, and 'special rights.'[50]

Lesbian, gay, and queer studies

The popularity of biological theories of sexuality was not the only sign of growth in sexuality studies in the late 1980s and early 1990s, quite the opposite. There was an explosion of interest in lesbian, gay, bisexual, transgender, and 'queer' studies, influenced particularly by the writings of Michel Foucault across the humanities and social science fields, which contributed to making Foucault one of the most influential philosophers of the twentieth century.[51] In *The History of Sexuality*, Volume 1, Foucault had questioned the naturalness and psychologization of 'sexuality.' There he called for a shift away from questions about desire in favor of an understanding of bodies and of pleasures that would not presume a psychoanalytic or psychological subject who stood behind them. Foucault was similarly anti-essentialist in his understanding of power. Sexuality's relationship to power should not be understood primarily in terms of degrees of repression, but through the production of *discourses* about 'sexuality,' discourses which literary scholars and historians could unearth and deconstruct. At stake in such Foucualdian endeavors was not 'liberation,' but moves *within* power: Foucault warned that all claims about 'natural' sexualities that might exist outside of power were false promises that only *seemed* to move outside of fields of power (and were to be interrogated as a ruse of power itself).[52] As Halperin notes, Foucault's shift away from liberation to survival tactics fit well with the politics of AIDS activism, which had moved beyond liberationist claims to engagement with biomedicine to extend the limited life spans of those who pursued it. With slogans such as 'drugs into bodies' ACT UP were not so much calling for anything like gay liberation, but for an understanding of bodies, pleasures, and practices that went beyond the epidemic of stigma that had anxiously attempted to protect 'the general public.'[53]

Queer theory also responded to the vexed ways that nature *or* nurture theories, claims about categories *or* continua, and emphasis on sexual identities *or* acts had all become available points for homophobic politics in the 1980s. Sedgwick argued that understandings of sexuality were primarily organized by framing the homo/heterosexual binary as a matter of determinative importance for a small minority or of universal relevance. Moreover, she asserted the epistemological importance of the homo/hetero binary in modern cultures, arguing that it structured other seemingly more basic binaries such as nature/nurture, cognition/ignorance, and male/female. Accordingly, the strategy was to develop anti-homophobic theory that did not flounder over concerns about epistemological purity in terms of seemingly independent distinctions which were, in reality, structured by homophobic impulses.[54]

Judith Butler drew upon speech act theory to resolve the dilemmas created by speaking about a category of people, such as 'women,' by asserting that all such speech acts were *performative* speech acts that called into being – with varying levels of success – the categories that they named and the identity of the speaker who did the calling.[55] Butler's account of identity subverted the traditional priority accorded to bodies and 'sex' and such actions as coming out or doing gender. She noted that discourses about physical sex were organized by speech acts, and as such could be conceptualized as effects of culture (albeit powerful and difficult-to-detect kinds of effects). Over the 1990s, new journals including *Sexualities*, *Journal of the History of Sexuality*, *GLQ*, *Journal of Gender Studies*, and *Sexuality Research and Social Policy* made 'sexuality' into a far less exclusively 'psychological' object of concern.

Although Foucault engaged substantively with the origins of psychology as a discipline, psychology researchers engaged but little with queer theory for some time. For radical feminists Celia Kitzinger and Sue Wilkinson, queer theory's critique of identity politics leaned too close to individualism.[56] Sandra Bem drew upon Judith Butler to query whether social transformation in the area of gender was best resolved by 'turning the volume down' on gender, as in her earlier work valorizing androgyny, or turning it up, allowing a multiplicity of queer genders to flourish.[57] I drew on Butler's theory of speech acts to examine how discourse – rather than any pre-social bodily materiality – might be responsible for the popularity of authors such as Simon LeVay.[58] Historian Henry Minton argued that queer theory could contribute to psychological theory by shifting emancipatory strategies away from grand narratives to immediate concerns, an ethics based on self- and social transformation rather than on the inclusion of static identity categories, an incorporation of dialogical practices into research, and 'a position of inquiry that is decentred from the norm.'[59] But such engagement with queer theory by psychology researchers was rare in the 1990s. More typical was the opinion expressed by John Gonsierek, in the preface to the first book in the APA series on lesbian and gay psychology, who described the new lesbian and gay studies as 'politically correct foolishness' on a 'fast lane into obscurity and irrelevance.'[60] Given this lack of engagement with queer theory, Hammack and Windell's critique of psychology's involvement with the law at this time as 'a quest to expand the concept of normality to include same-sex attraction, behavior, and identity, rather than to challenge the very idea of *normality* itself' is not surprising.[61] Nor is it surprising that they look to the broader field of lesbian, gay, and queer studies for alternatives. They describe the critique of same-sex parenting studies by sociologists Judith Stacey and Timothy Biblarz (2001) to support their conclusion that psychologists overplayed the strategy of emphasizing sameness and understated the uniqueness of same-sex relationships. Accordingly, I consider psychologists' engagement in parenting cases next.

Defending parents in court

In Chapter 2, I described early research and legal activism regarding lesbian parents. By the early 1990s, news reports made lesbian and gay parents more visible to many Americans, and psychologists estimated the number of children who were being raised by lesbian and gay parents to be in the millions.[62] Self-help psychology urged US lesbian mothers away from sources of collective support and created unrealistic ideals for coping alone. Few lesbians or gay men who parented sought recognition of their rights by the state, but in the 1990s, same-sex couples increasingly sought *second-parent adoptions* to ratify the parenting rights of non-biological parents. When they did so, they were assessed against heteronormative definitions of family, and were more successful in court when their private lives accorded with them.[63] Sodomy laws supported legal inequality. In the case of *Loving v. Loving* in 1985, the Virginia Supreme Court had ruled against allowing visitation rights for a gay father on the grounds that his relationship with a man constituted 'flaunting' of his sexuality and risked harm to his children. At their worst, psychologists colluded with this system. The 1991 COLGC survey of APA members included one response from a psychologist that described how 'a lesbian client whose son was the identified patient was told to move her "friend" out of her home because it was harmful to her son's sexual identity.'[64]

Lesbian- and gay-affirmative psychologists recognized the dilemmas created by defending individual families whilst reinforcing the heterosexist norm that led to undue scrutiny in the first place. Reviewing the literature on lesbian and gay parents, developmental psychologist Charlotte Patterson echoed Herek et al.'s

(1991) sentiment about privacy, describing as heterosexist 'the belief that everyone is or ought to be heterosexual' and such questions as 'Won't the children of lesbians and gay men have difficulty with sexual identity? Won't they be more vulnerable to psychiatric problems? Won't they be sexually abused?' as homophobic.[65] Recognizing that these questions singled out lesbian and gay parents as a discrete and insular class, Patterson and others nonetheless pursued the strategy of *answering* rather than *critiquing* these questions to achieve parents' rights.

The APA filed its first two amicus briefs in custody cases in 1995. In *Hertzler v. Hertzler*, Pamela Hertzler's rights to visitation were curtailed by her ex-husband Dean Hertzler and his new female partner, Christine Thompson, a firm Christian.[66] In *Bottoms v. Bottoms*, Sharon Bottoms was a young lesbian whose own mother claimed custody rights over her grandson, and was granted those rights on the grounds that he was being raised by two lesbian parents. In these and three other parenting cases prior to *Lawrence*, the APA forwarded the evidence that the sexual orientation of parents made no difference to children's psychological outcomes in any domains, and that the courts erred in allowing the sexual orientation of parents to sway their judgment.[67]

Neither judgment was overturned, although Dean Hertzler's opposition to Pamela Hertzler's access to her children had softened by the time their case reached the Wyoming Supreme Court. The Supreme Court of Virginia continued to deny Sharon Bottoms custody of her son. Virginia had a sodomy statute in place and the court ruled that Bottoms' lesbian identity assured that she would be conducting criminal acts in private such that her son's best interests were served by his grandmother's custody. There is a strong norm in US law as elsewhere to presume that parents are the people best placed to represent the best interests of their children. By refuting the prejudicial belief that lesbians and gay men harm their children, Patterson and other psychologists hoped to remove one plank from the argument that lesbians and gay men be denied ordinary rights to parent their own children. But as Pershing pointed out, in other cases, the Virginia Supreme Court allowed parenting rights to such parents as a stepfather who had killed his child's natural father, a father who had abused and murdered his wife, a man who had forced sexual relations with his daughter's half-sister, and a mother who had abandoned her children for several years.[68] None of these parents was deemed to have breached standards of morality or risked harm to their child as much as had Sharon Bottoms. The unprincipled homophobic ideology of the court remained considerable.

In January 1995, Patterson edited a special issue of the APA journal *Developmental Psychology* on sexual orientation. It included several articles emphasizing biological determinants of sexual orientation in childhood, and one meta-analysis of studies replicating the finding in *Sexual Preference* linking childhood gender behavior with adult sexual orientation.[69] Three studies examined adolescence, and centered on the timing of the emergence of same-sex desire, disclosure to friends and family and its consequences, and initial same- and opposite-sex behavior. A paper by Kitzinger and Wilkinson examined the discourses of sexuality used by women transitioning from heterosexual to lesbian identities.[70]

Other studies on adults concerned relationships and parenting. In her introduction, Patterson wove these articles into a developmental narrative, which, like the order of the articles in the volume, moved from prenatal hormones to gender-nonconforming childhoods to adolescent confusion and risk, to successful coupled adulthood.

The volume represents a landmark in the advance of lesbian and gay-affirmative perspectives out of the marginal journals and into one of the APA's most prestigious and well-read venues. Several of the articles in this special issue were cited in amicus briefs. For example, an article on the sexual orientation of the children of gay fathers led by Michael Bailey was cited in the brief for *Hertzler*,[71] and an article on the influence of prenatal hormones on sexual orientation by Meyer-Bahlburg was cited in the brief for *Romer*. In a closing commentary on the special issue, Diana Baumrind noted that three policy questions now dominated: the nature–nurture question, the risks to adolescent health, and the question of whether the sexual orientation of parents mattered.[72] This special issue also seems to re-entrench the norms established by Hooker's NIMH Task Force that sought to protect gay and lesbian adults from Queteletian normalization, but left the open season on gay kids to the biologists and the psychiatrists. In her introduction, Patterson lauded the diversity of essentialist and constructivist orientations drawn together in the volume, describing Green's longitudinal study, discussed in Chapter 2 above, as 'pioneering.'[73] Only as they passed variably through stages of assembling same-sex desires, identifications, and practices, in adolescence or in later adulthood, would such children enter the affirmative narrative.

In evaluating this strategy of focusing on demonstrating the normalcy of same-sex parents rather than challenging 'normality' in broader terms, it is important to consider that the APA was increasingly challenged by Christian right groups after the 1996 *Romer v. Evans* decision. After 1996, such groups relied less on voter initiatives in curtailing movements for gay and lesbian rights, and sought other strategies.[74] One response was a defensive reaction to the perceived threat that lesbians and gay men posed to 'the family.' Appeasing such conservative interests, President Clinton passed the federal Defense of Marriage Act (DOMA), signed into law in September 1996, which limited marriage to opposite-sex couples. Section 3 of the Act specified:

> In determining the meaning of any Act of Congress, or of any ruling, regulation, or interpretation of the various administrative bureaus and agencies of the United States, the word 'marriage' means only a legal union between one man and one woman as husband and wife, and the word 'spouse' refers only to a person of the opposite sex who is a husband or a wife.[75]

This federal act limited actions within states to recognize same-sex unions. Three couples filed for marriage licenses in the state of Hawaii in 1990 and Hawaiian courts ruled in 1993 and 1996 that the state could not discriminate by denying them marriage licenses. DOMA rendered such victories at the state level pyrrhic. After the Act was passed, several states enacted bans on same-sex marriage, particularly those states with conservative citizens and where laws now recognized anti-gay hate crimes.[76] *Romer* dealt a blow to attempts to generate new laws with clearly anti-gay *animus*. A defense of marriage and the family was one way to add legitimacy to anti-gay sentiment.

Another strategy was to contest the scientific status of the APA briefs themselves. As feminist psychologists had long recognized, arguing for group similarities in psychology is a tricky business, because our methods of statistical testing in psychology have been oriented towards reporting group differences as significant findings and similarities as null results.[77] Father and son team Paul and Kirk Cameron, of the Family Research Institute exploited this epistemological advantage by describing the APA briefs in the *Bottoms* and *Hertzler* cases as unethically overstating confidence in empirical similarities. They noted that Michael Bailey's paper on gay fathers and a recent follow-up study of lesbian mothers in the UK suggested that children raised by gay and lesbian parents might be somewhat more likely to question heterosexuality themselves. Drawing on the link between childhood gender conformity and adult sexual orientation in *Sexual Preference* and similar studies, they further noted that differences in children's play preferences in some studies could reveal 'incipient sexual orientation differences,' and concluded that children raised by lesbians had impaired interpersonal relationships.[78] In response, Herek wrote a compelling chapter describing errors in Paul Cameron's work as 'bad science in the service of stigma,' noting issues with his understanding of sampling, response rates, questionnaire and interviewer bias, and drawing publicity to unpublished findings.[79] Unsurprisingly, larger studies drawing on the National Longitudinal Study of Adolescent Health were later conducted by Patterson and her colleagues and confirmed that there were no psychological harms caused by being raised by same-sex couples.[80] As Victoria Clarke discussed, this challenge and response made visible that lesbian and gay psychology now not only had to consider the ontological question of what 'sexuality' was and what kind of a group 'lesbians, gay men, and bisexuals' were, psychologists also had to engage in boundary work as to what did, and what did not count as 'good science' in psychology.[81]

Hammack and Windell (2011) point to the work of sociologists Judith Stacey and Timothy Biblarz as more exemplary of work that challenged normativity than fit lesbians and gay men within its terms. Like Clarke, Stacey and Biblarz described the psychologists' 'no difference' position as an ideology, prompted by the institutionalized discrimination it faced, and insisted that the existing psychological studies failed to fully exploit lesbian and gay parents as a 'natural laboratory' for 'exploring the effects and acquisition of gender and sexual identity, ideology, and behaviour.'[82] Like Cameron, they concluded from a review of the existent literature that children of lesbian parents were more likely to be open to, and to have experienced, same-sex sexuality. Unlike Cameron, they also concluded that self-esteem and psychological well-being were higher among such children, if anything the children of lesbians and gay men were enhanced, and not impaired, by their unusual upbringing. Such differences might originate in several factors including lesbians' disinterest in enforcing gender through play preferences, and the liberal environments in which lesbian-headed families were likely to live might have the effect of 'broadening of children's gender and sexual repertoires.'[83] In essence they claimed that the kinds of group differences psychologists had argued against existed, and were a matter of sociological interest.

Stacey and Biblarz certainly challenged 'normativity itself' in ways that lesbian and gay psychology research on parenting had not dared to do. The review has since been assimilated into the APA's amicus briefs, but it initially had complex effects. In Ontario, Canada, the cases of *Halpern v. Canada* and *MCCT v. Canada* tested the validity of marriage licenses previously granted to same-sex couples. Although the couples in these cases had no children, two conservative scholars – demographer Steve Nock and psychologist Craig Hart – used the Stacey and Biblarz review to contest the 'no difference' argument regarding parenting, relying on Cameron's work to assert that the heterosexual nuclear family was the ideal formation and contesting the psychological studies for their lack of nationally representative samples. In an affidavit, Stacey and Biblarz replied that the sampling standard was not suitable in psychology and invoked Herek's rejoinder to Cameron. The plaintiffs won, making Ontario the first jurisdiction in North America to recognize same-sex marriage. But as these events demonstrate, articulating the normative creativity of lesbian and gay parents at this time, as Stacey and Biblarz surely did, remained a risky business. The homophobic edifice of the law was considerable, and the most effective engagement against it was not simply the one that voiced the most explicit or broadest anti-normative view.

Lawrence v. Texas: from immutability to harm

The 2003 Supreme Court decision in *Lawrence v. Texas* represents the watershed moment in this history. As in *Bowers*, this test of state sodomy laws hung on the arrest of two men, John Lawrence and Tyron Garner, who were having sex in private. But *Lawrence* was contested in Texas where sodomy law pertained only to homosexual acts. Several cases since *Bowers*, such as *Bottoms*, make it perfectly clear how sodomy laws created inequality in the private sphere by forbidding the expression of private sexuality. As Hammack and Windell note, the APA brief articulated the now familiar themes of normalcy, equivalency, and the harms caused by unfair law. In a section on 'The Development of Sexual Orientation,' the APA asserted an agnostic position on the causes of sexual orientation, asserting that sexual orientation emergences early on, often without previous experience, is resistant to psychiatric efforts to change it, and that such change attempts cause harm. Gone was any mention of the biological studies that undergirded the 'argument for immutability' in the Colorado Amendment 2 case; biological essentialism was no longer essential.[84]

The basis for ruling the Texas sodomy law unconstitutional mattered. Only one justice voted that the Texas law was unconstitutional because it violated Lawrence's right to Equal Protection. Five other justices opposed it as a violation of the 14th Amendment's due process clause. The due process clause ensures that states cannot deprive persons of 'life, liberty, or property' without due process of law. The United States Constitution does not mention privacy explicitly, but privacy rights had come to be interpreted under the rubric of 'liberty' to which due process could apply. Previous cases had extended liberty to the rights of unmarried couples to access contraception with privacy and for women to secure abortions privately. *Lawrence* included same-sex relationships within this legal remit. The judges also refused to particularize the sexual acts that it defined as private, allowing adults the *privacy* to define the boundaries of sexual and non-sexual conduct without demeaning people with the burden of saying before the law, in public, how they drew such lines. The judges understood themselves to be equalizing access to privacy to 'value-forming and value-transmitting relation-ships,' irrespective of whether those relationships occurred in marriage or could lead to procreation (even those that seemed highly unlikely to lead to relationships at all such as the acts between John Lawrence and Tyron Garner in question). American adults now universally enjoyed the liberty to define and practice *sex* as they wanted to, regardless of how the state, or their neighbors, defined these matters.[85] As Diamond and Rosky note, in so doing, *Lawrence* guaranteed a federal legal right to privately *choose* whether or not to engage in sex and loosened the need to define as discrete and insular – the group of people who were harmed by laws that prohibited same-sex conduct.

The *Lawrence* decision located the primary harm caused by sodomy laws not in the criminalization of sexual acts per se, but in stigmatizing and demeaning of a couple who engages in them.[86] Hammack and Windell (2011) note that this recognition that unfair law unfairly harms, not only through the law but through demeaning *stigma*, represents the single most important influence of psychology on the judgment. In overturning *Bowers*, the judges noted its historical inaccuracies. Far from having 'ancient roots,' they learned from lesbian and gay historians that old sodomy laws were rarely exercised, and that sodomy laws which singled out *homosexual* sex dated only from the 1970s. Far from requiring gay men and lesbians to define themselves as a discrete and insular group to achieve equality, *Lawrence* sought to move beyond a recent tradition of pointing to same-sex relationships as requiring particular legal prohibitions. In court, arguments for the Texan law proposed a legitimate interest in promoting morality. The majority of the judges disagreed. The fact that the sodomy law was traditionally viewed as moral was not sufficient to uphold it now, nor a reason to burden those it singled out with infringements of their private pursuit of liberty.

Considerable time had passed since *Bowers*, and the court recognized also that a change in social attitudes towards sexual minorities had occurred in the interim. Lawrence Tribe, who litigated the *Bowers* case, noted that the Supreme Court at the time of *Bowers* would not have accepted the kind of 'no difference' arguments about the commonness, normalcy, or equivalence of homosexual and hetero-sexual acts that the APA marshalled, and which were accepted in *Lawrence*.[87] *Lawrence* also represents a rare moment when the US Supreme Court looked *internationally* for precedent. *Bowers* had placed the United States behind the European Court of Human Rights which had first ruled against the exercise of a sodomy law, in the case of *Dudgeon v. United Kingdom* (1981) several years before

Bowers.[88] The position that a Judaeo-Christian or European heritage warranted state sodomy laws was unsustainable in 2003 when similar laws had been successfully challenged in Europe a generation earlier.

Minority stress and marriage after *Lawrence*

After *Lawrence* research on heterosexism increasingly focused on the manner in which stigma harmed sexual minorities, and the American Psychological Association quickly aligned around the fight for same-sex marriage which *Lawrence* opened up. As noted above, in the early 1990s psychologists had begun to take increasing account of the implications of heterosexism for mental health, particularly in studies of LGB youth and of adults victimized by hate crimes. Coming out became conceptualized as an important event with consequences for self-esteem,[89] and community psychologists began to theorize such concepts as *gay-related stress*.[90] The concept that stuck was Ilan Meyer's *minority stress* formulation. For Meyer, minority stress was an overarching explanation of group differences such as the finding that lesbians, gay men, and bisexuals were 2.5 times as likely as their heterosexual counterparts to develop a mental illness over their lifetimes.[91] Meyer introduced the term in 1995, drawing on its earlier use in the 1970s in relation to ethnic minority stress.[92] In the intervening years, social psychological studies had shown that ethnic minority folk did not have the lowered self-esteem presumed by the minority stress framework.[93] Meyer considered the term better suited to sexual minorities, in part because differences in socialization might result in differences in self-esteem and vulnerability to stress: 'LGB individuals do not have the benefit of growing up in a self-enhanced social environment similar to that provided to Blacks in the process of socialization.'[94]

Minority stress fit with the post-*Lawrence* era for three reasons. First, it brokered the guarantee of privacy that *Lawrence* provided to sexual minorities. It foregrounded the need to explain group differences in mental health, with an awareness that heterosexist prejudice still existed and would attribute such differences to inherent pathology. Of course, the minority stress framework shifted the default attribution to social causes. Second, minority stress created a social rationale for addressing these inequalities as they evidenced that the basis for the pursuit of liberty and happiness in private was far from equal, and for social reasons. Third, the theory articulated different ways that minority stress might feel and be experienced, opening up subgroup and individualistic analyses of differing reactions to minority stress ranging from resiliency to internalized homophobia. Meyer consciously invoked the growth of research on internalized homophobia, and cited critics such as Kitzinger who had drawn attention to the dangers of this concept. Bisexual young people were well represented in studies of youth at risk and several subsequent reviews have suggested that bisexual people have different, and often worse, mental health epidemiology than lesbians and gay men.[95] Minority stress and the harms that it causes provided a rationale to make bisexual people as central as if not more central than lesbians or gay men to the project of LGB psychology. Meyer's review rapidly became very well cited and crystalized a post-*Lawrence* understanding of how heterosexist harm moves from social structure into the individual.

The APA's pursuit of marriage equality also re-positioned the *same-sex couple* rather than the lesbian, gay, or bisexual *individual* closer to the center of the field. *Lawrence* opened up the ground for same-sex marriage. If two people could have sex in private because that sex might be, or might become, an intrinsic part of an intimate relationship, the reasons to deny that couple state recognition of such an intimate relationship appeared more dubious.[96] Prior to *Lawrence* there was very little interest among psychologists in same-sex marriage. But the study of same-sex relationships had continued to grow since the early studies reviewed by Watters in the late 1970s and early 1980s. In the early 1980s, Blumstein and Schwartz conducted an extensive study of same- and opposite-sex couples that was revolutionary in normalizing the study of same-sex relationships in sexology.[97] Later in the 1980s, psychological research by Lawrence Kurdek documented both similarities in the factors that lead to satisfaction and dissatisfaction in same- and opposite-sex relationships, and more egalitarian division of household labor in same-sex couples.[98] In its brief for *Lawrence*, the APA drew on the findings of Peplau, Blumstein, and Schwartz, and Kurdek to argue that same-sex couples were common, strong, and strengthened by the expression of sexual intimacy in private.

Opinion about the value of marriage within lesbian, gay, bisexual, and queer communities varied enormously. Ironically, one of the first studies of relationships captured by Morin's (1977) review concerned a couple's enactment of a same-sex marriage ceremony. Many same-sex couples continued to affirm their relationships in commitment ceremonies, both before and after DOMA, but attempts to file marriage licenses in the 1970s and 1980s were rejected.[99] Marriage became politicized in the 1990s, and had strong proponents among conservative gay authors who argued it might 'civilize' or 'tame' same-sex sexuality (particularly sex between men).[100] Similar arguments were sometimes aired in court by social scientists, in response to heteronormative standards assumed in family law. For example, in 1996 in *Baehr v. Miike* in Hawaii, sociologist Pepper Schwartz testified, and was challenged that in *American Couples*, she had found that same-sex couples were more likely to break up than were opposite-sex couples. Schwartz defended her position by noting that her research had been conducted prior to AIDS, and that AIDS had made people more cautious, less likely to have multiple partners, and more likely to settle down.[101] Other lesbian, gay, and queer theorists adopted the more radical ideology that emphasized that marriage is an inherently unequal state and its pursuit a short-sighted response to the threats that queer people faced, and that its pursuit of 'normality' blunted the edge of queer and feminist politics.[102]

Marriage, like the military, appeared to anchor a homonormative ideology that might give wealthy White gay men a place at the table of privilege, or access to equality, whilst prioritizing these goals would increase inequalities along lines of race, class, and sex.[103] Irrespective of these concerns, same-sex marriage had, by 2003, been recognized in the Netherlands (2000), several regions of Spain (2001–2), Belgium (2003), and Canada (2003). Within the United States, marriage also came to define the relationship between state and federal rights because of long-standing principles to recognize marriage licenses issued in one state in all others. In 1999 a case in Vermont led to a ruling that same-sex couples must be granted the same rights as married couples, but not marriage per se. Couples began entering Vermont 'civil unions' in 2000, but DOMA ensured that their unions had no legal recognition in their home states. In 2003, President George W. Bush drafted a failed constitutional amendment to define marriage as a union between one man and one woman. By the end of 2003, the state of Massachusetts had begun to issue *marriage* licenses to same-sex couples.

Social scientists began to take a far greater interest in same-sex marriage also around 2003. By the first years of the twenty-first century, fewer heterosexual Americans were in marriages than in earlier generations but marriage remained an aspiration of most young people, whose achievement could be seen as the successful expression of one's individuality.[104] Opinion polls show that support for same-sex marriage hovered at or below 30% throughout the 1990s but increased after 2003, particularly when same-sex marriage was framed as an *equality* issue.[105] Public opinion always showed more support for granting rights to same-sex couples under the framework of 'civil unions' – as in Vermont – rather than 'marriages' – as in Massachusetts and overseas.[106] In a clever social psychology experiment showing the symbolic politics of 'marriage,' hetersosexual participants deemed a state law allowing 'marriage' more threatening to their rights and status than one allowing 'civil unions.'[107] These findings evidence reactive distinctiveness; some heterosexual people might only notice and value the privilege of being allowed to marry each other when the distinct privilege they enjoy becomes threatened by a move for equality.[108] *Lawrence* not only protected sexual minorities from the burden of defining themselves as a discrete and insular group, it also forced the recognition of the implicit complement of this logic – that heterosexual people were a particular group, who enjoyed particular, unacknowledged advantages, that were both traditionally unexamined and difficult to justify when singled out for scrutiny.

In 2004, the APA issued three simultaneous statements on sexual orientation regarding marriage rights, parents and children, and rights to serve in the armed forces.[109] The resolution on Sexual Orientation & Marriage emphasized 'that it is unfair and discriminatory to deny same-sex couples legal access to civil marriage and to all its attendant benefits, rights, and privileges' less than two weeks after Bush's Federal Marriage Act failed to pass in the House of Representatives.[110] Following these resolutions, Division 44 put aside its fight with the Division for Military Psychology and focused on the marriage fight, and in 2005, in the case of *Li v. Oregon*, the APA submitted its first amicus brief on a marriage case (eight more would follow by the end of 2008). Nine couples had filed a lawsuit for same-sex marriage licenses on grounds of fairness and equality, but lost their case because a voter-led initiative had amended the state's constitution to define marriage as between one man and one woman. The amicus brief drew on familiar ground from earlier cases about the normalcy of same-sex couples, bolstered now by new estimates from the 2000 census that there were about half of a million same-sex households in the USA.[111]

The briefs also demarcated science from pseudoscience, based on standards accepted in the field, critical evaluation and peer review, and an acknowledgment that scientists often discuss limitations of their own research. The 'no difference' position was now stated in a manner that not only relied on scientific evidence but shifted the burden of proof towards providing valid evidence of 'difference':

> Scientific research cannot prove that a particular phenomenon never occurs or that two variables are never related to each other. When repeated studies with different samples consistently fail to establish the existence of a phenomenon or a relationship between two variables, researchers become increasingly convinced that, in fact, the phenomenon does not exist or the variables are unrelated. In the absence of supporting data from prior studies, if a researcher wants to argue that two phenomena are correlated, the burden of proof is on that researcher to show that the relationship exists.[112]

In the years that followed, the APA also supported several cases concerning adoption and fostering rights of lesbian and gay people. In contrast to the parenting cases prior to *Lawrence*, the same-sex couples were successful in these adoption cases.

In addition to arguments based on a lack of psychological differences, human rights provided a second ground for arguing for marriage rights that was of increasing international importance in the twenty-first century. In 2002, the World Health Organization became the first transnational global organization to cohere upon definitions of 'sexuality,' 'sexual health,' and 'sexual rights' that might support claims for state recognition of equal marriage, transgender rights, and other LGBT concerns.[113] Unlike other issues on which the APA had engaged, same-sex marriage was much more clearly an international issue, and one in which the United States could not be said to be leading. Celia Kitzinger and her wife Sue Wilkinson argued that UN human rights frameworks constituted a better grounding for equal marriage than arguments about 'no difference' and the psychological harm caused by minority stress. Consistent with Hammack and Windell's criticisms of the APA legal strategy, Kitzinger and Wilkinson argued that the contribution of scientific studies to social change was low, and most likely a step on a journey of progress toward the proper recognition of the sociological nature of inequality.[114] However, their attempt to broker a human rights argument in the UK to have their Canadian marriage recognized as a marriage rather than as a Civil Partnership was rejected in the UK courts. The judges asserted that marriage was 'traditionally' defined as that between a man and a woman, and demanded that Kitzinger and Wilkinson pay a punitive fine. Same-sex marriage was later introduced in the UK, through parliament, in 2014.[115]

Same-sex marriage presented dilemmas for feminist psychologists around the world who welcomed equality and the recognition that marriage would provide to lesbians and gay men, but also noted that marriage represented an *idealization* of relationships that historically privatized pain, violence, and suffering.[116] In making the argument for the harm that marriage *inequality* caused, APA briefs described marriage as providing benefits that same-sex couples could not access.[117] As such, work that supported equal marriage described same-sex couples as members of a discrete and insular class affected by a particular inequality. But campaigns for equal marriage did not simply serve the good of all same-sex couples, or all members of diverse sexual minority communities equally. Where marriage law has been equalized, men have used it more than women, often to stabilize property rights. Psychological research also documented LGBT people's ambivalence in welcoming the equality that state recognition of same-sex marriage brought, but remaining ambivalent about the effects of availability of marriage on social norms in same-sex relationships and LGBT communities.[118] As one might expect from a reading of Kitzinger (1987), attempts to *measure* attitudes to same-sex marriage with surveys revealed the liberal humanist orientation that characterized the dominant pro-marriage case. For example, radical queer critics of same-sex marriage, such as Michael Warner,[119] might have agreed with items on Pearl and Galupo's measure of attitudes to same-sex marriage such as 'Same-sex marriage undermines the meaning of the traditional family' and 'I oppose the legalisation of same-sex marriage.'[120]

Beverly Greene described the landscape of same-sex marriage as prone to divide-and-conquer politics that exploited tension by interpreting evidence of homophobia in Black communities as evidence that those communities were *inherently* anti-gay.[121] Polls showed that in the 2000s, African-Americans were, on average, more religious and observant, and were also, on average, more resistant to public arguments in favor of marriage equality.[122] After a voter initiative in 2008 in California nullified same-sex marriage licenses previously granted in that state, media focused on race differences in voting patterns, overstating the extent to which the outcome was driven by African-Americans and other ethnic minority voters.[123] But as Greene has pointed out, many African-Americans have bitter memories of analogies to their oppression from members of more privileged groups and promises of coalition that end in disappointment.[124] I think Greene is absolutely right to isolate the difference between reasoning about inequality by analogy and the real work of intersectional analysis and politics. Whilst analogies between equal marriage and the end of state bans on interracial marriage were common, many African-Americans had reasons to resent a shifting understanding of the goals of social equality, as discourses about the ideal family were often *unchallenged* by arguments for marriage equality, and such norms had long been used against African-American families.[125] Indeed, in the early 2000s, many poorer African-American women were targeted by a policy that *encouraged* them to get married so that they might be less likely to claim state support, even whilst efforts were being made to write the denial of same-sex marriage rights into the US Constitution.[126] Moreover, as marriage equality was pursued in the twenty-first century, and provided same-sex couples access to some standard ways of protecting parenting and property rights, income inequality continued to increase, in the United States and around the world, to levels that were unknown in the lifetimes of most people.[127] Economic volatility threatened many people's families, privacy, and dignity more than unequal law did. Turning up the volume on marriage equality was vulnerable to being one challenge to norms that 'identify one way in which we are different' which we assumed 'to be the primary cause of all oppression, forgetting other distortions around difference, some of which we ourselves may be practicing.'[128]

However, it would be wrong to consider that those who pursued marriage equality with the greatest determination were unaware of or uninformed by these problems. For example, as Celia Kitzinger noted in interview with her wife Sue Wilkinson and historian Jacy Young, 'So you had a critique of it at the same time as you got caught up in it.'[129] Esther Rothblum conducted important research by comparing those couples who went to Vermont seeking civil unions to their coupled siblings. However, Rothblum was also ambivalent about the priority marriage achieved:

> I don't know what to say about all these couples that are going to get married. I don't mind eating their wedding cake and going and hugging them, but you know it is just bizarre to me. That has been kind of a funny thing. Of all the important things facing lesbians and gay men and bisexuals, *marriage*? The other issue is the military. I would have never thought we would be killing ourselves to get into the military.[130]

Conclusion

Any understanding of the relationship between psychology and the law in the United States in recent times in which lesbian and gay psychology does not play the central role is necessarily impaired. By placing this relationship in its disciplinary context, I emphasized here how psychologists particularly contributed in making manifest the reality of the harms of *stigma*. The use of biology to undergird argument from immutability was not central to this argument, as *Romer* and other cases demonstrated. Rather, the recognition that lesbians, gay men, and bisexuals were vulnerable to being singled out as a discrete and insular group was pivotal. And singled out they were from the mid-1990s onward by a counter-science which contested the arguments in the APA briefs. In the next chapter, I examine this relationship among anti-gay *animus*, arguments about immutability, and the treatment of lesbians and gay men as a discrete and insular group in the context of research on attitudes and public opinion.

The successes of this strategy in its own terms are considerable. The strategy required those engaged in it to stifle valid critiques of the heterosexist reasons for the very existence of the questions that they were required to answer in court. Whilst this strategy could be seen as sacrificing a larger critique of normativity to achieve more circumscribed ends, I think that this legal activism can also be thought of as a far more queer kind of strategy. Minton emphasizes how queer strategies aim not at grand narratives but at strategies of resistance. The engagement in legal activism could be considered a kind of response to Sedgwick's call to marshall anti-homophobic theory even at the expense of epistemological purity. Moreover, by making the realities of heterosexist prejudice clear and working to reduce them, lesbian and gay psychologists played a part in creating a climate for *Lawrence* that was markedly different from that of *Bowers*. Psychologists were wise to notice that the courts are not the ideal context in which to contest normality whole cloth, but to do the piecemeal long-term work of unpicking it thread by thread. When compared with other disciplinary perspectives on sexuality, psychology's facting strategy has not fared badly in terms of its longevity and achievement in the domain of sexual orientation. 'There has always been a core of folks in APA and in its structure who work towards social justice, and that's really important,' recalled psychologist Beverly Greene:

> To be a part of something that becomes part of an amicus brief that APA files on behalf of some discriminated-against group to me is the highest calling, I suppose, in terms of how we use research; that it's not there just to feed the intellect but it's there to make the world better in some way.[131]

Notes

1   www.apa.org/about/offices/ogc/amicus/index-issues.aspx
2   American Psychological Association (2009).
3   Hammack & Windell (2011, p. 240).
4   Pope (2012, pp. 19–20).
5   Diamond and Rosky (2016).
6   Lee & Crawford (2007).
7   See e.g., Danziger (2006).
8   Wilkinson (n.d.).
9   Diamond and Rosky (2016, p. 373).
10 Bersoff & Ogden (1991).
11 Bersoff & Ogden (1991, p. 951).
12 See Benjamin & Crouse (2002); Clark, Chein, & Cook (2004).
13 See Eskridge (2002) for details by state.
14 Bersoff & Ogden (1991).
15 www.apa.org/about/offices/ogc/amicus/uplinger.pdf
16 www.apa.org/about/offices/ogc/amicus/bowers.pdf
17 See www.apa.org/about/offices/ogc/amicus/bowers.pdf, pp. 22–27.
18 See Coates et al. (1988), Herek & Glunt (1988), Melton (1988).
19 Herek & Glunt (1988, p. 890).
20 Coates et al. (1988, pp. 863).
21 *Bowers v. Hardwick*, 478, U.S. 186 (1986, pp. 192–196).
22 Halley (1993).
23 See Berube (1990) on experiences of early servicemen, and Grob (1991) on the development of the *DSM* from the army codes. Herman (1995) provides evidence that the proportion of those who were denied service on psychiatric grounds was far higher in the USA than in other countries engaged in the armed conflicts of World War II.
24 Herek (1993).
25 www.apa.org/about/offices/ogc/amicus/benshalom.pdf; www.apa.org/about/offices/ogc/amicus/watkins.pdf
26 Bersoff & Ogden (1991, p. 954).
27 www.apa.org/about/offices/ogc/amicus/watkins.pdf

28 Fox (1992).
29 See the text of Herek's statement here: http://psychology.ucdavis.edu/rainbow/htm l/miltest2.html. See also Herek (1993).
30 Burks (2011).
31 Belkin & Bateman (2003, p. 2).
32 See www.apa.org/about/offices/ogc/amicus/watkins.pdf, pp. 2–3; www.apa.org/a bout/offices/ogc/amicus/benshalom.pdf, p. 2.
33 Green (1988).
34 Bailey & Pillard (1991), LeVay (1991), Hamer et al. (1993). For early criticisms of this work from feminist biologists see Hubbard & Wald (1993), Fausto-Sterling (1992).
35 See Conrad and Markens (2001); Terry (1997).
36 Dorner (1976).
37 Barber (2007), Hire (2007). This organization changed its name to the Association of LGBTQ Psychiatrists in 2015.
38 See Zucker & Spitzer (2005).
39 American Psychiatric Association (1991).
40 Drescher (1998, p. 20).
41 Drescher (1998, p. 15–16).
42 Both my own early analysis (Hegarty, 1997) and Diamond and Rosky's (2016) more recent analysis have relied on Halley (1994), as does the discussion that follows here.
43 Herman (1996, pp. 139–140).
44 Drescher (1998).
45 Mucciaroni & Killian (2004).
46 Halley (1994, pp. 509–515).
47 Halley (1994, pp. 514–515).
48 Kimmel & Browning (1999).
49 Herman (1996, pp. 151–159).
50 See for example Morrison & Morrison (2002), Raja and Stokes (1998).
51 See Jagose (1996), Turner (2000).
52 Foucault (1978).
53 Halperin (1995).
54 Sedgwick (1990).
55 Butler (1990, 1993).
56 Kitzinger & Wilkinson (1994).
57 Bem (1995).
58 Hegarty (1997).
59 Minton (1997, p. 349).
60 Gonsierek (1993, p. ix). Thankfully this situation has changed, and for a developed account of how contemporary queer theory and psychology might intersect, see Johnson (2015).
61 Hammack & Windell (2011, p. 240).
62 See Falk (1989), Lewin (1993, p. 188), Patterson (1992).
63 See Connolly (1996, 1998).
64 Garnets et al. (1991, p. 968).
65 Patterson (1992, p. 1038).
66 http://law.justia.com/cases/wyoming/supreme-court/1995/123280.html
67 www.apa.org/about/offices/ogc/amicus/hertzler.pdf; www.apa.org/about/offices/ ogc/amicus/bottoms-brief.aspx
68 Pershing (1994, pp. 319–322).
69 Bailey & Zucker (1995).
70 Kitzinger & Wilkinson (1995).
71 Bailey et al. (1995).
72 Baumrind (1995).

73 Patterson (1995, p. 5).
74 See Herman (1996).
75 Defense of Marriage Act, The (1996).
76 Soule (2004).
77 Hare-Mustin & Marecek (1990).
78 Cameron & Cameron (1997).
79 Herek (1998).
80 Patterson (2006).
81 Clarke (2000).
82 Stacey & Biblarz (2001, pp. 162–163).
83 Stacey & Biblarz (2001, p. 172).
84 www.apa.org/about/offices/ogc/amicus/lawrence.pdf
85 Tribe (2004).
86 Tribe (2004).
87 Tribe (2004).
88 Johnson (2015).
89 Savin-Williams (1989).
90 See Rosario, Rotheram-Borus, & Reid (1996), Rotheram-Borus, Hunter, & Rosario (1994).
91 Meyer (2003).
92 Meyer (1995).
93 See particularly Crocker & Major (1989).
94 Meyer (2003, p. 690).
95 King et al. (2008).
96 Tribe (2004).
97 Blumstein & Schwartz (1983).
98 Kurdek (1993, 2005).
99 See Lewin (1999) on commitment ceremonies and Eskridge (2002) on early marriage cases.
100 See notably Sullivan (1996). For an insightful critique see Warner (1999).
101 www.lambdalegal.org/in-court/legal-docs/baehr_hi_19961203_decision-hi-circuit-court, p. 12, item 79.
102 Yep, Lovaas, & Elia (2003).
103 Duggan (2003), Warner (1999).
104 See Cherlin (2004).
105 See Baunach (2011, 2012).
106 Brewer & Wilcox (2005), Olson, Cadge, & Harrison (2006).
107 Schmitt, Lehmiller, & Walsh (2007).
108 On such reactive distinctiveness see Jetten, Spears, & Postmes (2004).
109 www.apa.org/pi/lgbt/resources/policy/index.aspx
110 www.apa.org/about/policy/marriage.aspx. The policy also stated that 'The same-sex couples identified in the U.S. Census may include couples in which one or both partners are bisexually identified, rather than gay or lesbian identified.' The APA was increasingly aware that its affirmation of same-sex marriages would not contribute to the erasure of bisexual people.
111 For examples of such logic within the APA amicus briefs see the submissions in *Department of Human Services v. Howard*, in the Arkansas Supreme Court, 2006, www.apa.org/about/offices/ogc/amicus/howard.pdf; in *Re R.A. and M.A.* in the Maine Supreme Judicial Court, 2007, www.apa.org/about/offices/ogc/amicus/ra-ma.pdf; and in *Matter of Adoption of X.X.G. and N.R.G.* in the District Court of Appeal, Third District, State of Florida, 2010, www.apa.org/about/offices/ogc/amicus/xxg-nrg.pdf.
112 www.apa.org/about/offices/ogc/amicus/li.pdf, p. 5.
113 Parker et al. (2004).
114 Kitzinger & Wilkinson (2004).

115 Kitzinger & Wilkinson (2015, May 26).
116 Finlay, Clarke, & Wilkinson (2003).
117 www.apa.org/about/offices/ogc/amicus/li.pdf
118 See Lannutti (2005).
119 Warner (1999).
120 Pearl & Galupo (2007).
121 Greene (2009).
122 Sherkat, deVries, & Creek (2010).
123 Egan & Sherill (2009).
124 Greene (2009).
125 Cohen (1997b).
126 See Cahill (2005).
127 Picketty (2014).
128 Lorde (1984, p. 116).
129 Kitzinger & Wilkinson (2015, May 26).
130 Rothblum (2009, March 14).
131 Greene (2009, September 11).

5 Naturalizing and denaturalizing sexuality in public

In pronouncing judgment in *Lawrence*, Justice Kennedy noticed a reduction in societal heterosexism since *Bowers*. Here I examine whether the change in attitudes he referenced was affected by the 'argument from immutability,' and the sense that social psychologists made of this question. Whilst sexuality scholars were prolific in their criticisms of the new gay biology throughout the 1990s, more conservative gay spokespersons voiced the view because the homophobic prohibition of homosexuality makes no sense on the basis that homosexuality is a largely immutable trait.[1] A decade after queer theorists coined the term *heteronormativity*, Duggan cast such conservative views as *homonormative*: 'a politics that does not contest dominant heteronormative assumptions and institutions, but upholds and sustains them, while promising the possibility of a demobilized gay constituency and a privatized depoliticized gay culture anchored in domesticity and consumption.'[2] In contrast, Duggan suggests that gay/lesbian politics must be understood *historically*, as intersecting with the politics of race, class, and gender, and not in 'nature/nurture' terms.

How might psychological science play its interpretive part in this question? Through legal activism, lesbian and gay psychologists had a growing stake in positivist-empiricist social psychology or 'facting.' However, over the 1990s an increasing number of scholars adopted principled social constructionist positions that rejected psychology's positivist epistemology 'which assumes that phenomena are either A or B.'[3] This methodological and epistemological pluralism led to vexing dilemmas as to whether lesbian and gay psychologists should reject positivist empiricist methods altogether on social constructionist grounds, or use them strategically to combat homophobic policies through something like Pope's 'facting.'[4] Within these discussions, I have often argued that the critical potential of experimental social psychology is underestimated by seeing science only as a means of strategically presenting pre-formed arguments, and that the revolutionary nature of social constructionist scholarship can sometimes be overstated.[5] I develop these arguments here by examining what positivist-empiricist social psychology can say about the need for the argument from immutability in changing public opinion. In the United States of the 1990s, social psychology had long been shaped by ambitions to be an *experimental* science, that could isolate and manipulate variables and observe their effects on thought, emotion, and behavior.[6] Whilst this project had also long been challenged by historicist arguments,[7] in this chapter I presume a truth value to social psychology experiments. I mean this chapter to get dirty with the data in these experiments,[8] to experiment with what it might mean to let this kind of positivist social science 'play its interpretive part' in history rather than writing it off as insufficiently historicist, insufficiently constructivist, or insufficiently critical of homonormative science. Should the new biology be valued because it contributed to the reduction of homophobia in the 1990s? What happens when we allow quantitative social psychology to play an interpretive part in answering this question?

The second sexual revolution

There are very plausible reasons to conclude that the development of biological models of sexuality played a pivotal role in the fall in societal homophobia between the *Bowers* and *Lawrence* judgments. As Jennifer Terry has noted, both Simon LeVay and Dean Hamer managed to achieve previously unheard of status as openly gay popular scientists when the media celebrated their findings about 'gay brains' and 'gay genes' in the early 1990s.[9] Their achievement is not trivial; later in the decade, readers remained shocked by biographies that revealed that Alfred Kinsey was bisexual in his interests and choice of lovers.[10] HIV/AIDS had required gay and bisexual men to engage the biological sciences more than ever before, and the discovery of the HIV virus as a single identifiable biological agent had affected the epidemic of stigma by discrediting theories about the 'gay life-style' as the cause of AIDS. Beyond their use in court, and citation in popular newspapers as pro-gay, biologists' arguments were also constructed as danger-ously pro-gay in evangelical Christian churches, and undermined the rationale of groups such as NARTH who promoted conversion therapies.[11] Meanwhile at gay pride events, T-shirts with genetic slogans were visible in the early 1990s.[12] By the end of the decade large corporations implicitly referenced biology to niche market their products to gay consumers. In 1997, *The Advocate* ran an article that raised concerns about the bioethical issues raised by the new studies,[13] but by the end of the decade the magazine sold itself to its LGB readers as 'the magazine you were *born* to read.' In 1999, in San Francisco's gay Castro neighborhood, I often saw Subaru's advertisement for its new all-wheel drive system advertised with the slogan 'It's not a choice, it's the way we're built.'

Was this lean into biological theories creating a change in social attitudes? Recall that the General Social Survey had asked Americans about the morality of 'sexual relations between two adults of the same sex,' and about the civil liberties of homosexuals since the 1970s. The two questions are not the same: White respondents typically expressed less moral condemnation in the late twentieth century. Black respondents expressed more support for anti-discrimination laws protecting gay men and lesbians.[14] In 1997, political scientist Alan Yang noted that homophobia was falling by both measures – the proportion of GSS respon-dents reporting that homosex was 'always wrong' had dropped by 15% between 1991 and 1996, whilst support for equal treatment in employment and housing increased steadily. Public support for allowing gay men and lesbians the right to serve in the armed forces increased also by 19% between 1992 and 1996.[15] Moreover, the proportion of Americans who endorsed the theory that sexual orientation was under biological control increased in the 1990s. But Yang cautioned against drawing the conclusion that biology was a solid platform for lesbian and gay rights, pointing out that 'identity politics' strategies had shown their weaknesses in preceding decades.

These shifts were not isolated to the 1990s, but continued year-on-year after Yang's publication and for unusual reasons. Social scientists decompose changes in public opinion into *intra-cohort* changes in individual attitudes, and *inter-cohort* effects caused by the replacement of older cohorts with younger cohorts. Typically, these effects balance each other; people get more conservative as they age, whilst younger, more liberal cohorts replace older more conservative ones. From the late 1980s onward, inter-cohort effects changed tack such that Americans also became *less* homophobic as they got older. This shift was highly specific – there was no equivalent shift in attitudes toward premarital or extramarital sex. The correlates of public opinion also changed: education became less of a factor in predicting heterosexism, whilst age and religion became more important.[16] In the 2000s, changes in attitudes to same-sex marriage showed similar intra-cohort changes.[17]

Can biology make you gay-friendly?

Was Yang right to caution against the attribution that biology made straight people gay-friendly? In the 1970s and 1980s, a few scattered correlational studies had found that heterosexual people who believed that homosexuality was a choice expressed more heterosexist prejudice than those who believed that homosexuality was caused by biological factors.[18] In the 1980s, social psychologist Bernard Weiner and his colleagues developed an attributional theory of stigma that seemed to explain these and other correlational findings. Early experiments had shown that people help those in distress more when they do not seem to have been able to control their fate, and that seemingly uncontrollable causes of distress elicit more pity and sympathy, while controllable causes elicit more anger and hostility. Extending this attributional logic from helping those in distress to stigmatization, Weiner and his colleagues observed correlations between the extent to which specific stigmatized characteristics were perceived to be uncontrollable or controllable and the extent to which they evoked such emotions as pity, sympathy, and anger. Weiner and his colleagues found that manipulating participants' perceptions of the cause of an individual's stigmatized trait induced the predicted emotions.[19] For example, they described a person who had contracted HIV from a blood transfusion or from 'leading a promiscuous sex life,' and found the predicted emotions evoked by each hypothetical HIV+ person.[20]

As this example shows, social constructionism forced psycholgosts to become more articulate about the values that informed their experimental designs for a reason. Attribution theory failed to recognize Herek and Glunt's point that effective responses to HIV/AIDS stigma needed to challenge the homophobia upon which it was built. Subsequent applications of attribution theory to HIV leaned even further towards heterosexist assumptions when they defined HIV transmission from homosexual sex as more 'controllable' than HIV transmission from heterosexual sex.[21] In considering 'pity' to be a better reaction to stigmatized groups than 'anger' the theory also fell short of social psychology writing that emphasized that members of stigmatized groups do not simply devalue themselves or welcome pity from others.[22] The logic of attribution theory fit perfectly with the aspirations of the 'argument from immutability' that emerged in the post-*Bowers* years. So too did the weakness of assuming that pity was an adequate response to the lack of civil rights for lesbians and gay men, as some critics of the argument from immutability pointed out.[23]

Weiner's original paper did not examine heterosexism, but he drew the link between his theory and the biological theory of sexuality in later work.[24] The link was also forged by Bernard Whitley, who conducted a survey in which he observed a correlation between students' heterosexist attitudes and their beliefs about the controllability of homosexuality. Whitley ventured that teaching the biological theory in human sexuality courses might reduce students' heterosexism because 'textbooks in this area typically present a number of biological explanations – implying uncontrollability.'[25] As evidence of such correlations accumulated, so too did statements of how they might be the consequence of the effect of biological attributions on attitudes. Herek and Capitanio found the correlation in a study of Black heterosexual Americans' attitudes. As they found correlations between personal contact with lesbian and gay people among White but not among Black heterosexual people, they wondered if White heterosexual people might be learning the biological theory from their gay and lesbian friends, such that 'changes in such beliefs may be an underlying mechanism through which contact experiences affect intergroup attitudes.'[26] In 1993, *The New York Times* ran a story reporting that the finding was evident in Gallop polls.[27] The Gallop Foundation had been asking questions about causality since the 1970s, and the correlation did not suddenly occur in the 1990s, but rather only became *newsworthy* then.

Were you *really* contributing to the reduction of heterosexist public opinion in the early 1990s if you told your straight friends that biology made you gay? What if you were a teacher who assigned a textbook that taught the theory that homosexuality was caused by genes and hormones? Or did it just sometimes *feel* like that? Weiner's attributional theory allowed at least two different psychological interpretations of this correlation. First, his theory specified that attributions drive emotional responses, which is how Whitley, Herek and Capitanio, and others interpreted it. Second, Weiner specified that 'negative events or effects in particular initiate attributional search.'[28] In other words, if you were not heterosexist to begin with, then you might not think about what caused homosexuality at all. This interpretation of the theory was rarely foregrounded, but it echoed Kameny's suspicion that causal questions had dubious motivations behind them. Attributions to controllable causes might *rationalize* heterosexist attitudes or other stigmatizing attitudes by making them appear more justified, either to oneself or to others.[29] The correlation might come about for several different reasons, explaining why you might feel like you were changing others' attitudes by telling them you were born gay even if you were having no effect on them at all.

Every good positivist-empiricist psychology student learns what to do in a situation like this. An observed correlation between variables A (e.g, heterosexist attitudes) and B (biological beliefs) could have resulted from either an influence of A on B, an influence of B on A, an influence on both A and B from some other third variable (C), or some combination of all three processes. There is a clear advice taught in every first year psychology course I have ever seen: run an experiment to see if B changes when you induce a change in A. Several such experiments have tested whether changing attributions affects stigmatizing attitudes in regard to different stigmatized characteristics, and their results differ widely. For example, changing attributions has been shown to affect stigmatizing attitudes in the domain of anti-fat prejudice, but to repeatedly fail in the area of mental illness stigma.[30] In some domains attribution theory is falsified and in some domains it is supported.

In the 1990s, three published experiments tested the theory in regard to heterosexism and their results are telling. First, Piskur and Degelman (1992) asked volunteers from a liberal arts college affiliated with the Assemblies of God to read either an article about the 'hypothalamic structural differences between homosexual and heterosexual men' or an article on hormonal similarities, or were given no article to read. Women reported less homophobic attitudes after exposure to the article on biological differences than in the no-article control group. However, there were no differences in the attitudes of men in the two groups. Second, Pratarelli and Donaldson (1997) reported an experiment that found no impact whatsoever on attitudes of reading a text that supported the biological model v. one that focused on its weaknesses. In the third and final study, Oldham and Kasser (1999) measured a small group of students' homophobia before and after they read either an article about the work of Hamer and LeVay or an unrelated article. Again the texts had no overall effect on students' attitudes, but the authors found two unexpected effects. First, among students exposed to the biological article, biology majors reported the most negative attitudes. Second students who remembered *less* of the article's argument reported the least homophobic attitudes.[31]

These findings do not confirm a direct effect of attributions on attitudes. They don't prove that no such effect could ever exist, but they shift the burden of proof quite a bit. Their authors made occasional comments that suggested how a third, 'C' factor – social identity – might have led to the correlation in a way that attribution theory did not specify. Piskur and Degelman (1992) opined that men and religious students might be less 'open' to the biological theory than women and more secular students. Oldham and Kasser's results also suggested that students' prior knowledge of biology made them closed to the biological text. In other words, people do not receive the biological theory as if they had no pre-existing beliefs and attitudes, but rather made sense of it actively and in ways that are different from each other. A later study found a pattern of *biased assimilation*. Students with initially pro-gay or anti-gay attitudes read a textbook passage about the biological theory. Regardless of their initial beliefs, all students became convinced that the biological text supported their initial beliefs and strengthened their attitudes.[32] Far from being a magic bullet for reducing heterosexism, the biological theory was more like a fascinating Rorschach inkblot onto which a range of different meanings could be projected. The biological theory might have the effect of polarizing opinions, not softening them.

Informed by queer theory, Felicia Pratto and I began to research a wider range of beliefs that might map out the conceptual space between heterosexist attitudes and enthusiasm for the biological theory. I teased out measures of belief in the *immutability* of sexual orientation from beliefs about the *fundamentality* or *discreteness* of sexual orientation categories. Around the same time, social psychologist Nicholas Haslam and his colleagues developed similar research. We both found that belief in the discreteness of sexual orientation categories tends to be correlated with *higher* levels of heterosexism, whilst belief in immutability tends to go with lower levels of heterosexism. Haslam and Sheri Levy later developed more robust measures of these essentialist beliefs and a third belief that sexual orientation categories are historically and cross-culturally *universal*.[33] This work helps to explain why gay brain and gay gene theories sometimes feel like a political Rorschach test, as they at once affirm that homosexuality is immutable and that lesbians and gay men are a different 'kind' of person. Our thinking about double-edged essentialist beliefs was behind the curve in sexuality studies, but fit the times in which the argument from immutability was proving itself inessential in court, and courts recognized that sexual minorities could be cast as a discrete and insular group, and were vulnerable to being singled out for prejudice as a consequence.

The correlation-causation error continued to stalk this literature, and was in favor of the assumption that beliefs about choice and immutability were the cause of attitudes rather than the reverse.[34] In the late 1990s, I began to conceptualize an alternative explanation of the correlation in which B (attitudes) affected A (essentailist beliefs). I drew on Herek's thinking about attitude functions and the ever-present evidence of a presumption that the biological theory that refuted choice as an explanation of sexual orientation was an inherently pro-gay theory. Might it *express* pro-gay values to say that you believed in immutability and express *anti-gay* values to say that you didn't? The emergence of niche marketing of products to gay consumers by invoking the biological theory suggested that this had become the case. I conducted two-wave surveys with students in the USA (in 1998) and in the UK (in 2001). In the first wave, students reported their beliefs and attitudes as in many other surveys, and the correlation between belief in immutability and lower heterosexism was evident, and stronger in the USA. In the second wave I presented the essentialist beliefs again and asked students if each belief were more likely to be voiced by a pro-gay or an anti-gay heterosexual person. Their responses to these questions allowed me to group the students according to their personal judgments about the kinds of attitudes that beliefs about immutability expressed. In both countries, a correlation between immutability beliefs and attitudes was evident *only* among students who believed that those beliefs were unambiguously pro-gay. Among students who thought those beliefs expressed ambivalent attitudes, no correlation was in evidence.

Since then, other researchers have focused attention on the kinds of social identities that lead people to take on essentialist views about sexuality to a greater or lesser extent. In one unpublished experiment, Miller found that Christian students in the USA endorsed immutability and showed less heterosexist attitudes after exposure to an article on the biological theory, but only if they had first been convinced by an argument that being religious didn't require one to be homophobic.[35] Another study found that Christian students who were told that experts preferred the genetic theory of homosexuality subsequently reported more heterosexist. These authors interpreted this finding as a reaction against the genetic argument, assuming that the students had presumed that the genetic argument was inherently pro-gay.[36]

Juan Falomir-Pichastor has conducted several studies that examine how heterosexual men who are readily threatened by gay men show lowered homophobia when presented with the biological theory because it emphasizes the distinctness of group boundaries and believe in the theory *more* for defensive reasons when they are threatened with evidence that equality for lesbians and gay men is being achieved.[37] Thomas Morton and Thomas Postmes found an effect of social identity on essentialist beliefs among sexual minorities. When faced with the threat that their identities would be *denied*, LBG participants endorsed immutability beliefs more. When faced with the threat of *discrimination*, LGB participants endorsed them less.[38] All of these studies suggest that religion, gender, and sexual identity make an impression on both attitudes and beliefs, and on how people engage to resolve apparent tensions between the two.

Lest I be accused of a little biased assimilation of my own, let me point out that there are studies that seem to confirm attribution theory's point in this domain. In one recent study, Spanish students read about either a genetic or environmental theory of sexual orientation. The genetic text increased belief in the genetic theory but had no effect on homophobic attitudes. Students exposed to the environmental theory reported increased belief in the environmental theory and an increase in homophobic attitudes, but it's not clear if these effects were causally related.[39] In addition, there are also a few studies that show no effect of presenting arguments of biology or immutability whatsoever.[40] On the whole, the experimental evidence doesn't add up to the argument from immutability or to a confirmation of attribution theory's claim that changing essentialist beliefs leads to a simple reduction in prejudice.

Rather, the surveys and experiments extend the argument that we enact our social identities when we hold and express particular essentialist beliefs about sexuality. As Morton and Postmes put it, 'essentialism can be more than a belief; it can also be an argument that is expressed to support or deny particular forms of identity expression by the self and others.'[41] Contra to the investment of conservative authors such as Andrew Sullivan in this line of thinking, and more in line with Lisa Duggan's insistence on intersectionality and historicism, the social psychological findings on essentialist thinking converge on the importance of people's social identities in shaping the ways that people believe that sexual orientation is or is not under biological control. In the last chapter, I argued that the APA legal strategy had real merit by virtue of what it achieved in comparison to other approaches. By the same token, I think it is wrong to consider the biological theory 'strategic' as it seems to have no discernible effect on public opinion whatsoever that positivist-empiricist methods have yet detected.

Social psychological studies conducted with undergraduate students, who are more often included in such studies for reasons of convenience, cannot necessarily be scaled up to the general population; psychologists have been making this critique of each other's over-reliance on student samples since at least the 1940s.[42] In spite of Yang's early cautions, later analyses of public opinion polls tended to interpret correlational evidence of links between essentialist beliefs and heterosexist attitudes rather quickly as effects of the former on the latter. Haider-Markel and Joslyn constructed linear regression models of public opinion that showed that belief in a genetic basis of homosexuality predicted statistical variance in opinions about homosexuality that was not predicted by variation in respondents' education, age, political orientation, religious background, or personal knowledge of gay/lesbian friends.[43] However, they did not test the *reverse* of this model – that heterosexist attitudes might predict unique variance in essentialist beliefs, as Haslam and Levy did when they re-examined their survey data in their paper's footnotes. Gregory Lewis drew together twenty-four surveys conducted between the 1970s and the twenty-first century, and found that the strength of the correlation between support for gay rights and belief in genetics grew *stronger* in more recent surveys. Moreover, religion remains the primary predictor of refusing the biological theory in recent surveys. Lewis concluded that many people, particularly secular people and liberals, may have adopted their beliefs to fit their pre-existing stances in regard to the morality of homosexuality, but on their own, attributions and the biological studies 'did not shift many more minds' in the early 1990s.[44]

Instead, I think that very ordinary people may well have been the primary drivers of the drop in heterosexism from the late 1980s onward. Since the 1950s, social psychologists have often followed Gordon Allport in testing the claim that the experience of contact with members of an out-group reduces prejudice towards that group. Although the terms 'homophobia' and 'heterosexism' were not known to social psychologists in the 1950s. Heterosexism has been shown to be reduced by contact more than any other form of prejudice that social psychologists had studied.[45] Psychologists and others who have set out to create anti-homophobic interventions have also contributed to this reduction in homophobia, whatever their theory of homophobia's causes. Somewhat irrespective of the methods that psychologists have used to reduce prejudice, from Morin (1974) onward, such interventions achieved moderate success.[46] The most common interventions to reduce heterosexism whose effects psychologists have measured have involved contact in educational contexts. Students are not a good model of public opinion, but college students' attitudes are in and of themselves important. Both teachers who have promoted the biological theory and teachers who have ignored it have found attitude change in their classrooms; the biological theory is not the essence of such classroom interventions.[47] Psychology students in one specialist course in lesbian and gay psychology lost interest in questions about causes and the detection of sexual orientation and became interested in 'special topics' such as supporting people through coming out processes instead.[48] Should psychologists appeal to such textbooks and assert the biological theory for pro-social ends, as Whitley's comment about textbooks suggests we might? Into the twenty-first century, psychology textbooks continued to reference lesbians and gay men very little and almost exclusively in the context of nature–nurture debates about sexual orientation (and to almost never mention bisexual people at all).[49] Teachers who choose to teach about lesbians and gay men with respect seem to create change whether they agree with, refute, or neglect the biological theory.

It matters how we weigh up the contribution to social change that the biological theory of sexuality made. Since LeVay's study, the space occupied by the *psycho-* in modern cultures is increasingly supplanted by claims about the *neuro-*. As Rose and Abi-Rached point out (2013), the dominant narrative of the neurosciences over the last 25 years has *not* been determinism, but *neuroflexibility*, making the developing brain an ideological pivot point for the imagination of effective intervention. Early on, Sedgwick noted this disjuncture between biology and immutability: 'increasingly it is the conjecture that a particular trait is genetically or biologically based, *not* that it is "only cultural," that seems to trigger an oestrus of manipulative fantasy in the culture.'[50] Both neuroscientists and their critics can overstate the impact of neuroscience on public understanding; and both would do well to understand that – in the much advertised case of sexuality – the biological theory has little effect on public opinion.[51]

Accordingly, there may be some utility in arguing for the biological theory because of who does and who does not endorse it, even if it does not have the purported attitude-changing effects that attribution theory ascribes to it. Psychologist James Weinrich, who led gay-affirmative efforts in SPSSI through the 1980s, argued in the mid-1990s for the biological theory on the grounds that it had been prematurely rejected by the gay movement's enemies. But nature/nurture theories can flip in their politics, as Sedgwick noted. Weinrich warned: 'we can predict that the next generation of right-wing theoreticians will reject these views and simply assert that homosexuality is a genetic pathology (or if they're really smart, a multifactorial one).'[52] Weinrich's prediction was not far from the truth. Following the enthusiasm for the *naturalization* of sexuality as a pro-gay strategy in the 1990s, sexuality was increasingly *denaturalized* in the interests of 'freedom' in the first decade of the twenty-first century, and with very different and diverse political motives and effects.

The denaturalization of sexuality

By the end of the 1990s, it was apparent that the story that gay men's sexualities was under biological control – and hence nobody's fault – was not the most novel news story to tell about men who had sex with other men. The late 1990s saw a reaction against gay-affirmative therapy that appropriated its narratives. A series of advertisements in national newspapers attested to the fact that 'the truth can set you free' and that spoke for 'ex-gays' who had been through *conversion therapies*.

Religious programs oriented towards coming out of the homosexual lifestyle rather than coming out had been in existence since the 1970s, but the movement was often vulnerable to internal scandals, often prompted by its leaders coming out as gay or lesbian later on. In the late 1990s, Anne and John Paulk, a married couple who had both come through conversion therapy programs, loomed large in these accounts, and John Paulk would also later come out as gay.

Media attention brought ex-gays to a wider public. The Board of Trustees of the American Psychiatric Association clarified its position in 2000, to restate that homosexuality was not a disorder and that people should not be compelled to change their sexualities. That same year its annual conference was picketed by ex-gay protesters. Psychiatrist Robert Spitzer, who brokered the meeting with the American Psychiatric Association's Board of Trustees regarding the de-pathologizing of homosexuality in 1973, was sympathetic to the ex-gay critics.[53] Spitzer quickly conducted telephone surveys with people – mostly men – who had been through religious conversion therapies. Based on their own accounts, their sexual desires had shifted towards heterosexuality, and their capacity for enjoying heterosexuality had increased too. As is so often the case with controversial sex research that aims to give light to underrepresented experiences, the science provoked questions about the trustworthiness of the participants' accounts. Accordingly, in the debates that followed the line between political allegiances and scientific methodology blurred beyond distinction. Spitzer understood that his study would lead into such territory: 'There is no doubt about what the participants in the study reported. The key question is judging the credibility of their self-reports.'[54]

Spitzer presented the study at the 2001 meetings of the American Psychiatric Association the following year. The media devoured the ironic resonances with the history of de-pathologization in 1973, with Spitzer's centrality to both events anchoring the narratives. In 2002, psychologists Ariel Shidlo and Michael Shroeder wrote a 'consumer report' on conversion therapies, warning of their failures and harms.[55] The following year, Spitzer's study was published in *Archives of Sexual Behavior* by its second editor Kenneth Zucker. Like his predecessor Richard Green, Zucker specialized in the treatment of children identified as having Gender Identity Disorder in Childhood, itself a diagnosis that made young people vulnerable to being placed in conversion therapy programs by religious parents.[56] Zucker invited commentaries on Spitzer's paper which often described scientific questions of sampling, methodology, and alternative interpretations of the sense-making that the participants reported in their short phone interviews.[57] Spitzer could cite the Surgeon General, the American Psychiatric Association, the American Psychological Association and other bodies who had warned against the harms of conversion therapy in positioning his work as speaking for a marginalized and silenced minority within a minority. Joseph Nicolosi, the leader of NARTH, was 'grateful to Spitzer for giving a voice to ex-gays.' Others were not sympathetic, and Herek noted, 'it is disappointing that the *Archives* elected to publish it.'[58] As psychiatrist Jack Drescher noted, Spitzer's persona in the media coverage of his work mirrored that of the conversion narrative of the ex-gay participants in his study. To paraphrase, he once had been swayed by the 'gay agenda' but had now seen the light.[59] As noted above in regard to John Paulk, often prominent members of the ex-gay movement later leave the movement and become critics of it upon accepting their homosexuality. It is possible to look back on Spitzer's study as mirroring such an ex-ex-gay narrative as he has since published an apology in *Archives* for the harm that his study caused.[60]

Another media story from 2001 confirmed that the biological narrative had always applied somewhat more to White men. The media drew attention to Black men on the 'down low,' a term that had long referred to all kinds of cheating, but which quickly came to refer to a discrete and insular class of secretive African-American, HIV+ men, in relationships with women, and sleeping with men.[61] Keith Boykin links the emergence of this representation to news coverage of CDC statistics on the disproportionate number of Black gay men who were HIV+, and the need for an explanation of this statistic that resided within the men whom the statistics described. Black men 'on the down low' also explained high HIV+ rates among Black women, reiterating in a much more racially marked way an older stereotype of bisexual men as the bridge by which HIV crosses from gay men to the 'normal' population. As Boykin notes, the stereotype fueled and exploited fears of homosexuality and dishonesty. The accumulated social science literature tells a much less essentialized story. Unsurprisingly, some African-American men identify as bisexual, some have sex with both men and women, and some take more risks around HIV transmission when having sex than others do. But these three groups of men are not the same men; men on the 'down low' are not a discrete and insular group that can carry the explanatory weight demanded by high rates of HIV among African-Americans.[62] Rather, African-Americans remain vulnerable to being stereotyped as the effect to be explained when differences are to be accounted for.

Similar dynamics stalked the discovery of 'barebacking' and 'bug chasing' in the same year, that took the sexual behavior of men who had sex with men out of its context of practice to create a discrete and secretive subculture of men seeking HIV infection. 'Ex-gays,' 'the down low,' and 'barebackers' all responded to a public discourse that had moved beyond the denial of either homosexuality's importance or its centrality to matters of public opinion.[63] All responded to a desire to make sex between men newsworthy, even though such sex was no longer so universally morally condemned. News coverage of studies kept the moral dubiousness of homosexuality alive by raising curiosity about matters of fact and value, occluding the ways in which science impacted lives in sustained ways. As Boykin explains, the 'down low' phenomenon was, in part, a result of the reporting of HIV/AIDS as a series of 'events,' rather than as a sustained attempt to cover the epidemic consistently over the long term, or to sustain critical attention on the structural reasons why rates of HIV remained high among Black men who had sex with other men. Such media events prompted the urge to purify truth from stereotype among scholars, which in turn fed competing claims to 'expertise'.

'Experience' – personal, ethnographic, spiritual, erotic – can seem to purify truth from stereotype, and experience has become such a normative way of understanding how we go through time that to query it at all can appear like a collusion with oppression. But *experience* is not just a simple category that opposes other more corrupted sources of social influence. Studies of stigma and social identity have long warned of how token representatives of stigmatized groups' experience are coaxed forward with particular experience narratives.[64] Butler warned about the dangers of responding to such pressure and speaking 'as a lesbian' (even if you are one), because to speak quickly calls forth a category one claims to represent and to which one cannot possibly do justice.[65] Rather, speaking from experience only works to achieve recognition for some people and under some conditions. Whilst scientific evidence and personal experience can seem opposed, the common linguistic roots of the words *experiment* and *experience* remind us that empirical science originally depended upon the act of witnessing by credible individuals.[66] 'Experience' is normatively organized around events and narratives, but time does not pass for everyone in a way that yields experience, as indicated by anthropologist Robert Desjarlais' research among homeless people with mental health problems who just 'struggle along.'[67]

Nora Ruck has analyzed debates about controversies engaging evolution and gender in this period and concluded that their discourse revolved around appeals to traditional authority.[68] In sexuality, it was more often the case that a discourse stabilized in which some scholars were positioned as experts and some as outsiders with claims on particular experience, but these positions did not map onto heterosexist and gay-affirmative positions neatly in the ways that they once did. Rather, in early twenty-first century psychology, it was increasingly common to see very new movements, such as feminism and lesbian- and gay-affirmative psychology, positioned ahistorically as if they had long been dominant positions in psychology and society at large.

The most influential aspect of this twenty-first century denaturalization of sexuality over the long term focused on women. By the late 1990s, the argument from immutability had accumulated critics among feminist psychologists, for such obvious reasons that key studies included only men and failed to replicate among women, had erased the narratives of women who experienced choice and change in their sexualities, remained committed to the presumption that any psychological gender that was biologically encoded was a one-dimensional masculinity–femininity construct, and relocated any displaced 'blame' or 'fault' from gay men onto their mothers' bodies.[69] Dubious 'nurture' theories presented in reaction to the new biological theory were vulnerable to similar criticisms.[70] Psychologists turned away from essentialist models of men's sexuality that they presumed were 'mirrored' among women.[71] Consensus shifted from gender similarities to gender differences, as reviews in field-leading journals suggested that women's sexuality was inescapably more fluid, flexible, and plastic than men's.

As earlier feminist debates had elucidated, research on gender differences does not escape the dynamics of androcentrism simply by adding data on women to the mix. Two early research reviews on gender differences in sexual fluidity illustrate Bem's concerns that gender differences can be interpreted with respect to male-centered standards such that differences reside within women and are interpreted to women's disadvantage. In one large review by Michael Bailey and two younger colleagues, the authors bemoaned the lack of a clear measure of sexual orientation that would go beyond self-report. The authors' commitment to an androcentric epistemology in which men preceded women was explicit. They would not presume similarities, but rather use male-centered models as the yardstick for difference:

> Women's sexual orientation, and indeed women's sexuality, must be studied from a perspective that tests the applicability of a male model, rather than assuming its applicability, in order to develop a comprehensive model of women's sexuality.[72]

Another lengthy review by social psychologist Roy Baumeister adopted a nature/ nurture framework to consider various reasons why women's sexualities might be more plastic than men's. Confirming Bem's fears that differences would be interpreted to women's disadvantage, its conclusions included recommendations for policy makers as to how to engage with sexual politics in a manner informed by this gender difference:

> A society that needs a change in sexual behavior in order to survive or flourish would do better to target its messages and other pressures at women rather than men because of the greater difficulty in changing the sexual desires and habits of men.

Or more prosaically:

> To the extent that the road to utopia runs through the bedroom, social engineers may find that male inflexibility presents the greater problem whereas female plasticity represents the more promising opportunity.

Or more concisely: 'sexual compromise will be easier for women than men.'[73]

Both reviews taking stock of sexuality research in the early 2000s confirmed feminist anxieties that descriptions of gender differences can quickly lead to prescriptions that one sex must change to accommodate the other, and that women should do the accommodating. Both reviews could be read, generously, as aiming to give voice to under-represented *experiences* of women, but I think that both also show how the rhetoric of representing under-represented experiences does not necessarily work to the advantage of the newly represented group.

Indeed, there is considerable evidence that by the early 2000s, the fact that heterosexual men *liked* the idea of sexual fluidity quite a bit was being talked about more openly. There are few moments in the history of heterosexism research where prejudice against *lesbians* is more in focus than prejudice against gay men. But in 1997, Louderback and Whitley introduced the hypothesis that heterosexual men might be less prejudiced against lesbians than gay men because lesbians are perceived to have 'erotic value.'[74] Their surveys showed that, among men, the 'erotic value' attributed to lesbians explained more positive attitudes to lesbians than to gay men. I'm not at all convinced that the 'perceived erotic value' of lesbians is a magic bullet for prejudice any more than the theory that gay men are 'born that way' might be.[75] In the mid-1990s, a rather new and trenchant understanding of male sexuality had opened up in response to feminism at that time, often informed by evolutionary psychology and promoted in the new market for men's magazines, particularly in the UK where they were known as *lads' mags*. These magazines, to which young men often looked for scripts about sexuality and relationships, promoted a post feminist message and featured soft porn images of women, often in lesbian-like poses.[76] Young men – straight and gay – can distinguish such 'fantasy' lesbian content from 'real' lesbians and often perform their own sexual identities by showing that they can do so.[77] Psychologists often made sense of these developments through a concern for the 'sexualization of culture' and its effects on the disempowerment of women and girls in particular.[78]

By the late 1990s there were also new financial drivers to consider female desire as flexible and in need of repair coming from pharmacology. Psychologist and sex therapist and feminist activist Leonore Tiefer recalled the launch of Viagra in 1998 as a tipping point in the medicalization of sexuality. 'When Viagra was approved in 1998, people started talking about where is the Viagra for women? I thought that was a serious mistake.' Tiefer and her colleagues initiated the New View Campaign which tackled forms of medicalization that aimed to *create* distress among women about sexuality with the aim of marketing new medical solutions to those problems.[79] One of the dangers of gender differences research is that if *context* is not properly understood, then social differences can be seen as residing within the body. Tiefer's activism was similarly motivated by a concern that new drugs were being marketed as liberating for women at the same time 'that women don't have comprehensive sex education, not to mention abortion rights, availability and coverage for contraception, and safe contraception.'[80] In Breanne Fahs' interviews with American women in the 2000s, the opening up of sexual scripts in regard to fluidity was not simply empowering, but many women felt an obligation to perform a kind of 'compulsory bisexuality' for their heterosexual male partners.[81]

One set of studies garnered particular media impact in the early 2000s for shining a light on the way that people experience sexual arousal that you might not know from what they said about themselves or their 'experiences.' The studies fulfilled Bailey and his colleagues' desire to develop a way of assessing sexual orientation that undercut self-report by extending male-centered paradigms to women.[82] In these studies, women and men watched several two-minute clips of pornographic films of two men having sex and of two women having sex. In addition to reporting their arousal, participants' genitals were monitored for blood flow.[83] The authors recorded the difference in arousal responses to the film clips of women and of men having sex. They then graphed the relationship between this 'male-female contrast' and the participants' self-reported sexual orientation. Heterosexual and gay men showed a difference in male-female contrast to the films that you might expect; more to films of women for heterosexual men, and more to films of men for gay men; the essentialist model of male sexuality stood firm. Lesbian and heterosexual women showed much less specific patterns of genital arousal, being somewhat aroused by both kinds of films.

The findings suggested greater 'plasticity' among women, but also that male sexuality had a discrete nature; bisexual-identified men were mostly more aroused by the films of men than women, leading the authors to conclude that bisexual men showed more sex-specific arousal patterns than their sexual identities suggested. In a *New York Times* article titled 'Gay, Straight or Lying,' Bailey opined, 'I'm not denying that bisexual behavior exists … but I am saying that in men there's no hint that true bisexual arousal exists, and that for men arousal is orientation.'[84] In other words, bisexual people – or men at least – are fooling themselves and should make up their mind. The *NYT* article included several critical views in response to Bailey's and galvanized considerable response from bisexual scholars in psychology and elsewhere. The study also, incidentally, later failed to replicate. Nonetheless, these studies also contributed to a climate in which public stories about the psychology of sexuality were premised on the fact that gay people existed, and toyed with the question of whether it was reality or perception that other non-heterosexual kinds existed.

Like Baumeister, Chivers et al. made very different conclusions about how women and men should respond to evidence of their own responses to same-sex stimuli. By universalizing non-specific arousal among women but not among men, the authors came to very different advice about how to move from homosexual desire to homosexual identity for women and for men:

> A self-identified heterosexual woman would be mistaken to question her sexual identity because she became aroused watching female–female erotica; most heterosexual women experience such arousal. A self-identified heterosexual man who experienced substantial arousal to male–male erotica, however, would be statistically justified in reconsidering his sexual identity.[85]

In sum, these studies at once not only aimed for, and achieved, a way of describing other people's sexual orientations that undercut their claims to experience, they also used those claims to give advice as to how people should identify themselves.

Feminist research requires a higher standard of objectivity that goes beyond adding women to studies designed in androcentric ways, finding that results differ, musing about whether nature or nurture caused the difference, and musing about the advice that people should follow as a result. Psychologist Lisa Diamond went considerably further in her study of sexual fluidity at this time. In her oral history on the *Psychology's Feminist Voices* website, Diamond describes her early encounter with postmodern feminism that 'makes your brain hurt' and of developing scientific practices 'with a critical perspective that understands both the strengths and limitations of that mode of inquiry.'[86] I empathize with this recollection; reaching across from social psychology into queer theory to begin experimental research on essentialist beliefs and heteronormative explanations felt similarly brain-stretching.

Diamond began a longitudinal study of young sexual minority women's develop-ment, and was careful to disentangle, rather than to conflate, such factors as sexual identity, sexual desire, and sexual behavior. In an early paper, she demonstrated that the essentialist narrative that sexual minority women have 'tomboy' childhoods fit her data poorly.[87] Rather than simply add women to a male-centered model, Diamond theorized the evolution of sexuality in terms of loosely coupled gender-specific arousal and gender-general attachment systems that lead adults to fall in love with each other. By so doing she developed a different biologically oriented theory of sexuality in which women, not men, were the norm. Diamond under-stood the influence of attachment on sexual behavior to be mediated by oxytocin, a neuropeptide hormone whose effects are somewhat oestrogen dependent.[88] Her model of nature explained the experiences of her young women participants whose sexual identities changed following experiences – sometimes unexpected experiences – of falling in love with a woman or a man. It also explained the self-report of those who felt that no label worked because they were romantically oriented to one sex but erotically more aroused by the other.[89]

From nature/nurture to the sexualization of culture

This chapter has discussed the promises that both immutability and flexibility have held in psychology's engagement with the public about sexuality in recent decades. Can a historical understanding of sexuality act as a balm on the bruises that the binary terms of such discussions have imposed? There is a weak and a strong argument to the history of psychology. The weak argument goes that psychologists should understand their intellectual history. The strong argument insists further that psychological concepts themselves change over historical time, as Foucault insisted about 'sexuality,' for example.[90] Although framed in terms of our evolutionary natures and the influence of social stimuli, the research that constituted the twenty-first century denaturalization of sexuality confirms the relevance of the strong argument as surely as the interplay between public opinion and beliefs about immutability does. The dichotomy between nature and nurture – or fluidity and immutability, or flexibility and fixity, or reality and stereotype, or science and politics – may recur in psychology particularly because we have methods for understanding *natural history* (as encoded in our shared biology) and *recent events* (as when we examine responses to stimuli) but very little by way of understanding temporal events that happen over centuries, or even decades, that nonetheless affect the psychology of sexuality.[91] This problem is not solved by appeals to interactionism, any more than a job that requires a middle-sized screwdriver is an argument that alternating between or 'combining' operations with big and small screwdrivers will get the job done cleanly. Rather, it is an argument that we live in history, punctuated by non-transitive events such as legal decisions, changes in norms and attitudes, technological developments, and changes in patterns of what we consider reasonable to consume. In the first part of this chapter, I attempted to move beyond nature/nurture thinking by focusing on both changes in attitudes and beliefs over time and the sense that psychologists made of them. I conclude with some thoughts about how the denaturalization of sexuality in the twenty-first century might also be thought of as historical.

The studies from the Bailey laboratory exemplify a kind of research on responses to pornography that is uninfluenced by the emergence of porn studies, arguments that pornography is more than a stimulus that provokes a behavioral response, and that porn's meaning changes with genre, context, and the past history of the viewer.[92] Indeed, on reading these psychological reports, I wouldn't trust these authors to use their rigid categories of gender to find two-minute clips that would necessarily turn me, or anyone else, on or off. Students have not always been happy to have their genital arousal measured in the lab watching gay and lesbian porn, and researchers, ethics committees, reviewers, and journals have not always imagined that such practices could be scientific ways to study sexuality. In the 1960s, if men were shown homoerotic pornography by psychologists it was often in the service of curing homosexuality through aversion therapy or detecting homosexuals through pupil dilation or other physiological measures. In the 1980s, many male students saw pornography in psychology laboratories to see if it affected their sexism, objectification of women, or rape propensity.[93] Psychologists have shown women pornography in laboratories far less often, largely because they have always *presumed* very large sex differences in interest in and consumption of pornography. The studies' central findings supplant one gender difference story (women are uninterested in porn) with another (women are aroused by just about anything).

The studies also inhabit a zeitgeist characterized by concern among the public and psychological professionals about 'the sexualization of culture.' By the 2000 census a majority of Americans had home access to the internet.[94] Going beyond the 'weak' claim that the internet informed psychologists' views about how sexuality was changing over recent historical time, it seems reasonable to assume that the internet changed the meanings, practices, and norms of sexuality itself. Research on female sexuality fluidity and plasticity notably positions technologically mediated arousal close to or far from the category of the natural. The studies from the Bailey lab venture that watching pornography on screen is the royal road to the truth of human sexuality, a claim that would have made the participants – particularly the women participants – appear very peculiar in a less porn-friendly era. In contrast, in Diamond's work, it is the inherently human nature of sociality that allows romance to carry someone's desires over a gender boundary.

The digital mediation of sexuality makes many more people similar to the participants in these experiments than in earlier eras, but it is also insufficient to see the internet as merely 'representing' sexuality rather than changing the very human experience of it. Behind the sexualization of culture thesis is a fear that a pre-existing natural sexuality is in a process of rapid, unique, ongoing historical corruption. Whilst sexuality researchers may be motivated to deny that such change is happening, the internet is certainly enabling practices that put the schemas for understanding sexuality that preceded its emergence into a historical context. In spite of the considerable conceptual complexity of her work, Diamond ontologized sexuality in terms of its components such as identity, attraction, and behavior, as earlier researchers had done. Yet, in an age of online chat rooms and cybersex, consensual definitions of the line between 'feeling' and 'doing' are sometimes elusive and people can reasonably disagree about where attraction ends and behavior begins.[95] Such matters require us to think about how human history, often taken to originate with the invention of writing, impresses itself on human capacities that we imagine to be 'natural' (in the sense that they are species general and evolved). Alternatively, we imagine that such nature is only moderated by 'society' or 'culture' (variable dynamics that we can sample, control, or reverse at the moment). Rather, the human experience of sexuality may be changing in our twenty-first century time in response to distinct historical events, and in ways that – like most historical events – are not going to be simply reversed. Any alarm that is caused by the recognition that culture is sexualizing us at this point in history, seems augmented to the extent that we imagine that there is, or has been, a 'natural' sexuality outside of human history.

The internet not only affects the private and intimate but also the public. It is impossible to understand the interest in the down low or barebacking without thinking about online pornography, chat rooms, the concerns of those who were not using that online material about the sexual scripts they coaxed, or the validity of claims to speak from experience from those who inhabit those online subcultures (or at least said that they did). The fate of the ex-gay movement is also intertwined with the emergence of online writing forms, from the 2005 exposé on Zack Stark's blog of his experiences in an ex-gay program to the war of gay, ex-gay, and ex-ex-gay narratives of personal experience competing for your attention on *YouTube* and other sites. In very recent years Exodus International has moved attention away from coming out of homosexuality, focusing on 'sex addiction,' which is one way to name the experience that some people face when they watch more online porn than they are comfortable about. Historians are no different: in the 1990s, I spent some time copying newspaper articles on LeVay and Hamer's research from university microfilms. These days I can find artifacts such as the 2009 *NYT* article 'What do Women Want' reporting on Chivers' and Diamond's work from my smartphone, which will also tell me that it is one of the most downloaded articles on the *New York Times* website. Historians of psychology must do their job now in an era after 'decay time' in which the past is no longer imagined as crumbling in locked away, difficult-to-get-to archives, but is often remembered in public digital forms. There is so much more of the past to remember than any one human memory could feasibly hold. Accordingly, it is important that we examine critically the historical understanding of LGB psychology that we *select* as the basis for our understanding of how the field expands, moves forward, and fulfils Brown's vision to transform other areas of psychology.

Notes

1 Sullivan (1996, p. 47).
2 Duggan (2003, p. 50).
3 Brown (1989, p. 452). See DeLamatar & Hyde (1999).

4 Kitzinger & Coyle (2002).
5 Hegarty (2001, 2007a).
6 For a classic statement of this aim see Allport (1954).
7 See Gergen (1973).
8 Hegarty (2007b).
9 Terry (1997).
10 See particularly reactions to Jones (1997) described in Gathorne-Hardy (1998).
11 Herman (1996).
12 Terry (1997).
13 Gideonse (1997).
14 Lewis (2003).
15 Yang (1997).
16 Loftus (2001), Treas (2002).
17 Baunach (2012).
18 Aguero, Bloch, & Byrne (1984); Levitt & Klassen (1974); Schneider & Lewis (1984).
19 Weiner, Perry, & Magnusson (1988). For earlier research on altruism and on emotional responses see Piliavin, Rodin, & Piliavin (1969) and Reizenstein (1986) respectively.
20 Weiner et al. (1988).
21 Dooley (1995).
22 On self-esteem and stigma see Crocker & Major (1989) and for a critique of pity and attribution theory as applied to disability see Fine & Asch (1988).
23 Ordover (1996).
24 Anderson, Krull, & Weiner (1996), Weiner (1993).
25 Whitley (1990, p. 375).
26 Herek & Capitanio (1995, p. 103).
27 Schmalz (1993).
28 Weiner et al. (1988, p. 739), see Hegarty & Golden (2008, p. 1038).
29 For a discussion of such rationalization see Crandall & Eshleman (2003).
30 Crandall (1994), Corrigan et al. (2001).
31 Oldham & Kasser (1999), Piskur & Degelman (1992), Pratarelli & Donaldson (1997).
32 Boysen and Vogel (2007).
33 See Haslam and Levi (2006), Haslam, Rothschild, & Ernst (2002), Hegarty (2002), Hegarty & Pratto (2001).
34 Perhaps the most extreme example of this slippage is an article by Landén & Innala (2002) titled 'The effect of a biological explanation on attitudes towards homosexual persons: A Swedish national sample study.' There is no 'effect' in the paper, it reports only a correlational study. Even very strong papers in this literature show the presumption in favor of the theory that beliefs inform attitudes. In their important study of essentialist beliefs, Haslam and Levy (2006) observed race and gender differences in heterosexist attitudes, and tested group differences in essentialist beliefs and statistically mediated them, providing evidence that beliefs impact attitudes. In the body of the paper, the authors report several statistical analyses consistent with this conclusion, but in its *footnotes*, they report an additional eleven mediational analyses confirming that gender and race differences in attitudes might just as easily mediate race and gender differences in essentialist beliefs. These analyses were added at the request of a reviewer, and all of them were highly statistically significant results. Even the strongest and most influential papers in this literature show a systematic preference to interpret correlations first as evidence of effects of beliefs on attitudes and to consider other possibilities only second. By so doing, these authors also differentially reward the reader who takes the time to read the occasional long footnote.
35 Miller (2008).
36 Mitchell and Dezarn (2014).
37 Falomir-Pichastor & Hegarty (2014), Falomir-Pichastor & Mugny (2009).
38 Morton & Postmes (2009).

39 Frias-Navarro et al. (2015).
40 See also Hegarty & Golden (2008), Reimer, Kok, & Hospers (2014).
41 Morton & Postmes (2009, p. 658).
42 See for example Henry (2008), McNemar (1946), Sears (1986).
43 Haider-Markel and Joslyn (2008).
44 Lewis (2009, p. 683). This perspective also helps to explain the findings of authors such as Sheldon et al. (2007) who interviewed a broad cross-section of Americans about the likely positive and negative consequences of finding a gene that determined sexuality, and found that a sizeable proportion struggled to think of any positive or negative implications at all.
45 Pettigrew & Tropp (2006).
46 See Allport (1954), Bartos, Berger, & Hegarty (2014).
47 Hegarty (2010), Altemeyer (2001).
48 Hegarty (2010), Waterman et al. (2001).
49 Barker (2007).
50 Sedgwick (1991, p. 26).
51 O'Connor & Joffe (2013).
52 Weinrich (1995, p. 201).
53 Erzen (2006).
54 Spitzer (2003, p. 413).
55 Shidlo & Schroeder (2002).
56 Cianiotto & Cahill (2005).
57 See particularly Rind (2006).
58 Nicolosi (2006, p. 159), Herek (2006, p. 135).
59 Drescher (2006).
60 Spitzer (2012).
61 Boykin (2005, pp. 14).
62 Millett et al. (2005).
63 The events also intersected, as in 2002 the *Exodus International* newsletter began celebrating Black history month and reaching out more deliberately to African-American communities. See Erzen (2006).
64 Goffman (1963).
65 Butler (1991).
66 Scott (1991), Shapin (1995).
67 Desjarlais (1994).
68 Ruck (2016).
69 Veniegas & Conley (2000).
70 See the critique of Daryl Bem's (1996) 'exotic becomes erotic' explanation of sexual orientation by Peplau et al. (1998).
71 My language borrows from Blackwood's (1985) criticism of such assumptions in the anthropological literature on sexuality.
72 Mustanski, Chivers, & Bailey, (2002, p. 129).
73 Baumeister (2000, pp. 369–370).
74 Louderback and Whitley (1997).
75 Carmen Buechel and I similarly found a *positive* correlation between Louderback and Whitley's measure of the Perceived Erotic Value of lesbians and Herek's 'old-fashioned' measure of prejudice but a *negative relationship* between PEV and Morrison and Morrison's *modern* measures among UK straight men (Buechel & Hegarty, 2007).
76 See Taylor (2005) on lads' mags contents.
77 Hegarty & Buechel (2011).
78 APA Task Force (2007). For critiques see Attwood (2006); Evans, Riley, & Shankar (2010); Gill (2009); Epstein, Kehily, & Reynold (2012).
79 Tiefer (2001, 2005, October 31, p. 10 of transcript).
80 Tiefer (2005, October 31, p. 10 of transcript).

81 Fahs (2009).
82 Chivers et al. (2004); Rieger, Chivers, & Bailey (2005).
83 Chivers et al. (2004, p. 738).
84 www.nytimes.com/2005/07/05/health/straight-gay-or-lying-bisexuality-revisited.html?
    _r=0
85 Chivers et al. (2004, p. 741).
86 Diamond (2011, August 6).
87 Diamond (1998).
88 Diamond (2003).
89 Diamond (2008a, 2008b).
90 Foucault (1978).
91 See Pettit & Hegarty (2011) for a longer exposition of this argument.
92 Attwood (2006).
93 Hald, Semana, & Linz (2014). Indeed, research by Dana Bramel in the early 1960s
    that suggested that male students might have a 'latent' homoerotic response to erotic
    male stimuli was quickly written off as inherently unethical (Hegarty, 2013). See Gentile
    & Kinsman (2000) on the 1960s, and Linz, Donnerstein, & Penrod (1987) on the 1980s.
94 US 2000 Census.
95 Ross (2005).

6 Cisgenderism and affirmative LGBT psychology

LGB psychology has been, and remains, in a state of flux – and for good reason. The lives of sexual minority people, the social and cultural contexts we inhabit, and the means by which psychologists claim to generate knowledge about us continue to change. This change has not been simply 'progressive' – either in the sense of being an accumulation of scientific evidence or an unambiguous march of social progress. But the change that has been achieved through LGB psychology is considerable, and it is not a surprise that it has been represented as a particular progressive accomplishment to be celebrated – and to be *used*.

Whilst lesbian and gay psychologists in the 1980s and 1990s looked to the psychology of gender and race for paradigms, in the last decade lesbian and gay psychology has come to ground analogies of how transgender psychology might develop. The recent history of LGB psychology has also been taken to scaffold the expansion of an affirmative project to transgender people in the last decade. The promise of LGB psychology in this effort rests both on its decades-old institutional structures within professional psychology organizations, and the paradigm shifts away from medical models. This shift in lesbian and gay psychology's position from unfamiliar vision-to-be-dared to the familiar ground of a future vision is nowhere more clear than in the 2009 *Report of the APA Task Force on Gender Identity and Gender Variance*.

If lesbian, gay, and bisexual psychology could play a role in bringing about a more affirmative psychology for gender minorities, then it would be fulfilling, in part, the promise of Laura Brown's vision of a transformative paradigm. Optimism for such a transformation can draw our attention to hopes for the future and away from what the past has actually been. Throughout its development, LGB psychology has been stalked by descriptions of LGB cultures as static and unchanging across time. For example, Mays and Cochran (1988) critiqued 'safe sex' advice that reached poor ethnic minority women as reflecting the norms of gay culture, but in so doing erased the ways in which Callen and Berkowitz's (1997 [1983]) advice was a *rejection* of the gay culture of its time, and a call for its transformation (that many gay men rejected). From the late 1990s onward, popular stories about the psychology of sexuality have represented gay identity as something that is firmly accepted in American society as if it had always been there, even whilst sodomy laws limited liberty, many Americans considered homosexual relations to be always immoral, and the rejection of the ego-dystonic homosexuality diagnosis and conversion therapy remained recent and precarious achievements. One risk of using LGB psychology as the ground for LGBT psychology lies in the necessary assumption that LGB psychology has achieved more than it has, and by so doing contributing to modern prejudicial thinking that equality has been achieved. One gift that transgender psychology might give to LGB psychologists is the understanding of how analogies feel when one's group is so positioned.

The second risk of such an analogy is that it prioritizes LGB psychology as ontologically prior to transgender psychology, and by so doing not only overlooks the ways in which these LGBT people come to sometimes share common fates, but also prioritizes sexual minority over gender minority issues for no clear reason at all. In Chapter 2, I detailed how lesbian and gay psychology emerged from gay liberation. Such professionalization oriented 'lesbian and gay' initiatives around an apparently discrete group of people defined by their sexual object choice, overlooking the ways in which liberation from object choice and from gender itself were equally central to gay liberationist thought. Whilst counseling organizations for lesbians and gay men developed in the early 1970s and bore fruit into a developed literature by the 1980s, organizations for transsexual people floundered early on.[1] As transgender became a better-known identity term in the 1990s, some transgender theorists began to invest strongly in the evidence of experience, phenomenological understanding, and the representation of transgender people in the shaping of academic questions that concern transgender people.[2] Others emphasized that transgender was a broad umbrella category which might include lesbians, gay men, and bisexuals who also transgressed gender norms.[3] Given that gender identity disorder in both adults and children remained in the *DSM-IV* in 1995, both minoritizing and universalizing strategies seem warranted to me, and their contradictions more tolerable than the ideology that they jointly opposed.

Where was psychology in this moment? Organized lesbian and gay psychology, on its own, did not do very much to support transgender movements. There is no history of amicus briefs to describe, only very recent evidence of any paradigm shift towards demedicalization, and no special issue of *American Psychologist*, akin to those addressing HIV/AIDS, that make the health needs of transgender populations central concerns. The 1995 special issue of *Developmental Psychology* illustrates that the state of 'open season' on gay kids remained unchanged long after the perspectives, rights, and normalcy of lesbian and gay adults had been validated by psychological research and psychology associations. Psychologists by the mid-1990s remained firmly commited to essentialist assumptions about binary gender which the transgender movement of the 1990s challenged.[4] Relations between psychology and transgender communities were rendered more precarious still by the publication of and response to Michael Bailey's 2003 book *The Man Who Would Be Queen*. The history of this controversy has been written as one of a scientist who was unfairly subject to hostile attacks from transgender activists, but in a way that overlooks the fact that some of us psychologists articulated reasons to worry about Bailey's failure to follow any methodological procedures and to incur risks by so doing.[5] In 2005, when Nicola Tee and I attempted to publish her MSc work on attitudes towards trans people's rights in the UK – the first empirical research on the psychology of transphobia in Europe – the journal's action editor initially rejected it on the grounds that transgender was a sociological and not a psychological phenomenon.[6]

However, some members of the Committee on Lesbian, Gay and Bisexual Concerns shared doubts about the re-classification of Gender Identity Disorder (GID) as a mental illness in the *DSM-IV*.[7] In 2002 members of Division 44 were delivered a training in transgender issues by Kat Rachlin and Jamison Green.[8] Indeed, psychologists often remained very committed to a psychiatric paradigm for understanding transgender people into the 2000s. In 2005, Division 44 initiated The Task Force on Gender Identity, Gender Variance and Intersex Conditions. The committee received several requests for advocacy in challenging the removal of GID from the *DSM-IV-TR*, but it adopted a more collaborative approach such that its mission became that to 'assist APA in addressing transgender issues in training, education, research, and policy, including the specific needs of APA members, both psychologists and students, who identify as transgender.'[9]

In 2006, members of Division 44 were presented with the possibility of adding 'transgender' to the division's name. This expansion from LGB to LGBT was greeted with ambivalence. Some Division members voiced 'considerable enthusiasm,' others 'had reasons for remaining lukewarm.'[10] As with early lesbian and gay psychology, the first group whose concerns appeared to be addressed were *psychologists*. The Task Force also compiled a list of resources, conducting a survey of psychologists' experiences, and published an information brochure. The Committee on LGB Concerns changed its name to the Committee on LGBT Concerns (CLGBTC) in 2008, and the APA added gender identity and expression to its own employment non-discrimination policies in the same year.[11] The 2009 *Report of the APA Task Force on Gender Identity and Gender Variance* 'marks a historic occasion for the APA.'[12]

This Report is 'historic' also because it tells an account of recent history, and I want to comment on that account here. I do so out of concern that the 2009 Report overlooks concepts that have been tried and tested throughout the recent history of LGB psychology, which might be of greater utility to transgender psychology than those that anchor the Report. Whilst LGB psychology often advanced only after community-based organizations, activists, and individuals had made clear the lived reality of inequality, the Report here traces a history in which the contributions of ordinary people are underestimated relative to those of psychologists. Central to this approach is a failure to challenge medical models of difference and personhood, which continue to affect the people whom the Task Force initially hoped to address.

Ordinary people's capacity to create change is underestimated when the Report argues for a key role of the *disciplines* in improving the lot of transgender people:

> Studies emerged that approached transgender issues from such disciplines as psychology (e.g., Kessler & McKenna, 1978), anthropology (e.g., Bolin,

1988), sociology (e.g., Devor, 1997a, 1997b), and the humanities (e.g., Garber, 1992). And since the 1990s, a public health research agenda has developed in response to the impact of the HIV/AIDS epidemic on some segments of the transgender community (e.g., Bockting & Avery, 2005; Bockting & Kirk, 1999).[13]

In drawing this material together, the Report suggests a natural accumulation of evidence over ignorance, with psychology playing a primary role. But in so doing it leaves out the neglect of transgender issues in psychology's paradigms in recent history. The first citation to the book-length treatise *Gender: An Ethnomethodological Approach* by Susanne Kessler and Wendy McKenna (1978) is a case in point. This work was informed by teaching collaborations with transsexual people and the sociological method of ethnomethodology, which Kessler and Mckenna learned from Stanley Milgram at the City University of New York. Their work challenged the 'natural attitude' that there are two and only two sexes, that those sexes are defined by biology, and that any exceptions to these rules are a performance, joke, or mistake. Their work was used by some transsexual people in making sense of their experiences, but was virtually ignored by psychologists for 20 years. Its authors attributed the more recent appreciation of their work to the emergence of a distinct, visible successful transgender social movement in the 1990s.[14]

The Report does describe the history of the transgender movement, but it tends to very much downplay how historic change can emerge from the analysis of psychological experiences of marginalization. It describes the development of university-based treatment programs in the 1970s, their dismantling in the 1980s, and the Harry Benjamin International Gender Dysphoria Association/World Professional Association for Transgender Health (HBIGDA/WPATH) Standards of Care, describing how the dichotomous understanding of gender of medical treatment in the 1960s and 1970s remained unchallenged until an 'alternative paradigm began to emerge in the 1980s when Virginia Prince coined the term "transgenderist" to refer to males who live full time as women without undergoing genital re-constructive surgery.'[15] The Report does not make clear that Prince coined this term to describe her own experience.

The Report goes on to describe the contribution of Sandy Stone, 'a postoperative male-to-female transsexual, [who] was one of the first to call for transsexuals to come out and affirm their unique identity and experience "from outside the boundaries of gender, beyond the constructed oppositional nodes" of male versus female.'[16] Whilst acknowledging Stone's identity, the Report does not clarify Stone's accomplishments in cultural studies or other fields. A year before this APA Report was written Y. Gavriel Ansara introduced me to the concept of cisgenderism: the ideology that both marks and devalues those who do not identify with the gender assigned at birth.[17] There is something cisgenderist about this haphazard marking of authors as transgender or transsexual people, but never in particularizing people as cisgender in the Report. This asymmetric marking bears a family resemblance with LGB psychologists' understanding of heteronormativity, and the consequences of locating difference only in some groups. Why should people be considered trans or considered theorists but rarely both?

The committee consulted with several external organizations in writing the Report, including the American Psychiatric Association, which did not recognize transgender psychiatrists as experts. This is because 'it is not policy to have individuals with a disorder examining the *DSM*.'[18] The Task Force also consulted the World Professional Association for Transgender Health – an interdisciplinary body whose *Standards of Care* had since 1979 set the benchmark for the clinical management of sex reassignment and the Society for the Scientific Study of Sexuality, as well as social work and public health bodies. As this broad range of consulting organizations might suggest, the Report often draws together incommensurate paradigms:

> Research regarding oppressed and stigmatized groups ultimately has sociopolitical implications as well as the usual clinical ones; at times, politics and science seem to pull in two different directions, both appearing to be a significant feature of the research landscape. A case in point is the debate about whether GID should be a diagnostic category in the *DSM*. Although this is a question subject to scientific analysis, it is also a question of stigma, as is the debate regarding the biological basis of gender variance.[19]

It would seem that questions are being sorted through, so that we might be able to tell what is purely science or purely politics in the end. But things in psychology were not simply getting better by 2009. Y. Gavriel Ansara and I cataloged the abstracts archived in *PsycINFO* in the first decade of the twenty-first century that pertained to trans children. The abstracts routinely *pathologized* them, understanding their expressions of gender identity to be medical entities, and often *misgendered* them, writing about them by using gender identities assigned at birth even when there was empirical evidence that the children did not identify with them. Whilst we did find affirmative, constructionist, and empathic research on such children in this period, it was far less often *cited* than research which was conducted from within medical research contexts, and particularly research that was produced by authors who were associated with the most published author in the literature, psychiatrist Kenneth Zucker. To be fair, the Report notes that 'there is very little research and commentary on psychosocial issues for children and adolescents with gender identity issues, although that is slowly changing.'[20] However, as Kenneth Zucker was also one of the authors of the 2009 APA Report, we concluded that shifts in psychology would not be accelerated by the report's recommendations.[21] Rather there are examples of pathologizing and misgendering throughout its pages.

One of the insights that lesbian and gay psychology developed from feminism is the point that language matters. Ambivalence about transgender *identity* bubbles up through the Report *because* of the lack of progress in psychology even in recent history:

> The problem for the task force was that in reviewing the extant psychological research, we at times found ourselves using the same language and

reproducing a perspective that risked reifying the aspects of the research to which some transgender people (and some psychologists) so strenuously object. However, we believed that it was important to reflect the state of psychological research in order to support our recommendations.[22]

Language can be asked to do many things. Here, it is asked explicitly to keep the terms of discussion open, to escape strenuous objections, and to reflect what exists. Whose interests are pursued when these conflict-avoidant goals are prioritized over the affirmation of transgender identities?

Indeed, the discussion of transgender identity formation quite deliberately blocks analogies to LGB experiences. The Report notes that many transgender people rejected the closet from the 1990s onward but cautions that the term 'coming-out process from the LGB experience implies that the ultimate healthy outcome is to be out as a transgender person' and this adoption is not recommended on the grounds that it might be overly prescriptive.[23] The report offers no solution for transgender people who would conceal who they are, other than the psychiatric paradigm based on lying which Prince, Stone, and others found unworkable. Instead the Report discusses a model of familial coping with identity disclosure modeled on Kubler-Ross' stages of the grieving process, written from family members' perspective rather than that of transgender persons.[24] Given the reality of cisgenderist ideology and transphobic prejudice, I do not doubt that many family members experience the coming out of some family members as transgender as resembling grief in some of its aspects. Nor do I doubt that psychologists lack an adequate understanding of identity development of transgender people. Rather, I find the erasure of the long tradition of *critiquing* coming out models in LGB psychology to set an unnecessary limit on the affirmation of transgender identity. Why can such models not be critiqued for their cisgenderist limits as they have been critiqued for their androcentric and ethnocentric limits in the past?

In Chapter 2, I described how lesbian and gay-affirmative psychology developed at the same time as children who were described as gender variant remained subject to psychiatric treatments. The Report might have gone further as a contribution to LGB psychology if it had revisited this history when it attended to the issues facing gender-variant children. Rather, George Rekers' work from the 1970s was discussed without critique, and without reference to his principled opposition to lesbian and gay psychology on the grounds that psychologists should help parents to prevent homosexuality, transsexualism, and transvestism in the young.[25] Indeed, the sections of the Report on children evidence a sustained attention to questions about causality; they require a willful suspension of appreciation for LGB psychology's history of querying expert perspectives and experts' presumptions to ask questions about causality, if those sections are to be read with a clear conscience.

The Report continually notes that transgender people are subject to stigma that is analogous to that which lesbians and gay men experience and which psychology can address:[26] 'Studies of gay and lesbian people have demonstrated the negative impact of stigmatization ... therefore, it is not surprising that many markers of minority stress can be found in transgender populations.'[27] Accordingly:

> Much of what psychologists have learned about the respectful and appro-
> priate treatment of people who do not hold dominant-group status with
> regard to other dimensions of diversity will be broadly applicable to people
> whose dimensions of diversity involve gender-variant identity and gender
> expression.[28]

Prejudice researchers had by 2009 begun to document transphobia, with community based organizations again leading the way in producing the first reports,
and later researchers documenting the beliefs that occur with this prejudice. As in
the early literature that Morin reviewed, the acceptance of the *existence* of stigma
precedes the development of the 'special topics' literature.

However, as Kitzinger warned, individualist notions, such as stigma, can
rapidly be used as more benevolent forms of re-pathologizing people. The report
mentions critics of the diagnosis of Gender Identity Disorder in Childhood, who
had rightly pointed out that the distress that children feel can come not from their
gender identities, but from variable social reactions to those gender identities.

> However, the real issue is that children and adolescents who are extreme in
> wishing for or adopting a cross-gender role need assistance to avoid the
> negative impact of stigmatization and to ensure that whatever decisions they
> make, or are made on their behalf, about their gender role will ultimately be
> in their best interests.[29]

Here again the report is unknowing about the extent to which it is enacting the
normalizing dynamics that it seems to critique. It imagines a distinction between
normal and *extreme* desires for gender roles that is itself a normalizing binary. It
describes 'the negative impact of stigmatization' as if such stigmatization were
inevitable, and not something that mental health professionals could do something
about.

Research suggests instead that children who feel atypical within their assigned
gender only experience impaired well-being to the extent that they experience
pressure to conform to gender norms.[30] In the 2009 APA Report family therapy
models that work to address the impact of cisgenderism and heteronormativity on
parents' capacities to care for their children are described as 'providing a dissenting
perspective to the traditional treatment approach.'[31] The traditional approach in
question is the behavior modification practices that link Rekers', Green's, and
Zucker's work. Comparison of the children and parents who use such dissenting
family therapy models rather than behavior modification approaches in this tradition shows that the children in question exhibit equally gender-atypical behavior.
However, the parents who engage the 'alternative' approach have attitudes to
gender that are more liberal than usual, and their children's peer relations are
better than those children in 'traditional' programs. Accordingly, there were

grounds to consider family therapy models as more than 'dissenting views' by 2009. A behaviorist 'tradition' was allowed to continue to harm here, even after evidence of better alternatives was available.[32]

Finally, I wanted to discuss the report's failure to engage with psychosocial issues that affect the lives of intersex people. The Task Force originally considered intersex within their remit, but decided to exclude it as early as 2005. Yet intersex is very relevant here. John Money drew selectively on cybernetic theories to understand the unfolding of that which we understand as 'gender identity' in children, and his early work was cited in the 2009 Report as pivotal to modern understandings of 'gender.' Money organized a medical paradigm from the 1950s to the 1990s that urged health professionals to conduct 'corrective' genital surgery on infants, assuming that children would identify with their assigned gender, and could only live if unambiguously sexed as female or male. In 1985, he received a Distinguished Scientific Award for the Application of Psychology from the American Psychological Association, at which time his treatment paradigm was virtually unchallenged.

Studies of the gender and sexual identities of intersex children have long been deployed in biologists' debates about causes of sexuality. As it is unethical to alter the hormonal balance of human infants to investigate these biological theories, scientists have often looked to children with atypical hormonal levels, such as those with Congenital Adrenal Hyperplasia (CAH), to bridge the gap in their understanding of animal and human sexuality. Consequently, until quite recently, psychological research on people with CAH has been limited to nature–nurture research with no consideration of diversity or of psychological moderators or mediators at all. It is difficult to see what benefit, if any, people with CAH have garnered from being objects of such curiosity.[33] However, these theories often worked hand-in-hand with claims that the developing brain encodes sexual orientation and other supposedly gender-related traits.[34]

In the 1990s, Money's treatment paradigm came under increasing attack. In 1993, Cheryl Chase initiated the Intersex Society of North America (ISNA) in response to the biologist Anne Fausto-Sterling's popular article on variability in sex characteristics. Chase and other intersex activists used strategies of 'collective confrontation' by protesting medical meetings, borrowing slogans from ACT UP such as *Silence=Death* to do so. The exposure that Money's most celebrated case history was a case of fraud and abuse, arguments for a moratorium on early surgery, and increasing emphasis on the role of foetal androgens in organizing gender identity all ensured that Money's reputation was considerably reduced by the early 2000s. Instead an increasing number of people identified openly as 'intersex.' Sociologist Sharon Preves was the first to publish a study drawing on interviews with a large sample of self-identified intersex people, and she concluded that an identity-based movement was emerging that would continue to challenge shame and secrecy, in much the same way that LGBT movements had already done.[35]

Such social psychologically informed uses of the history of LGBT movements to understand the historical context of intersex were not mentioned at all in the 2009 Report. Instead, this history is glossed as one in which intersex and trans activists had briefly collaborated, but the collaboration was abandoned:

We also noted that the perceived linkage between gender identity concerns and DSDs that had developed during the late 1990s, when transgender and DSD advocates and activists routinely cooperated, had in recent years been deemphasized or discouraged within both the transgender and the DSD communities.[36]

The term DSD here requires some explanation, particularly as it certainly didn't exist in the late 1990s when 'DSD advocates' were supposed to have been doing these things. In the early 2000s, the leadership of ISNA began to move away from the term 'intersex' and direct confrontation towards diverse forms of what Georgiann Davis calls 'contested collaboration' with members of the medical profession. 'DSD' is an acronym for 'disorders of sex development,' and this term emerged at a pivotal event in recent intersex/DSD history: the 2005 meeting of experts in Chicago which resulted in a new 'consensus statement' on the management of these conditions. As Davis puts it, the consensus statement 'allowed medical professionals simultaneously to move beyond the John Money debacle and to respond to intersex activism and feminist critiques that were successfully claiming intersex was not a medical problem.'[37] Whilst the APA were content to defer psychological questions about intersex in 2005, pediatricians reframed these questions in psychological terms around the same time. The consensus statement recommended the formation of multidisciplinary teams, including psychologists, joint decision making about medical interventions with parents, and a shift in treatment towards maximizing the psychosocial well-being of the child.

Since the consensus statement, most of the well-funded international collaborations of the last decade have been biomedical in orientation with little or no input from psychologists whatsoever.[38] Matters which drove activists to protest, such as the protection of children's bodily integrity, the impact of normalizing and pathologizing language, clinicians' transparency about their intentions, uncertainties and actions with patients and their families, and ambiguity about the psychosocial outcomes of purely medical treatments remain ongoing concerns that have been amply documented by psychologists and others. Social scientists continue to emphasize, as they have now done for decades, that attempts to normalize psychological development via medical intervention is likely to fail; the intervention itself needlessly conveys the sense that the growing child's body is deficient, and it exerts normative pressure.[39] In all of this the thinking about normativity, voice, power, and the futility of focusing on questions about causality in the history reviewed in this book provide a set of historical resources for developing a range of practices that might undo the shame and stigma that intersex people and their families continue to report. However, the 2009 Report erases the history of the intersex movement and obscures any possibility of useful LGBTI theorizing in psychology. LGB psychology remains very relevant to the lives of people who might be addressed by the terms 'intersex' or 'DSD' by activist or medical actors in the present. In addition to the continuing use of people with CAH to keep nature/nurture theories of sexuality in play, doctors rely on a 'heterosexual paradigm' in understanding which kinds of medical interventions to pursue when they intervene with the aim of improving the functioning of intersex bodies.[40]

'Home' is a persistent metaphor that structures the 2009 APA Report: 'The institutional structures for sexual orientation are considered the obvious "home" for transgender issues,'[41] and 'Division 44 has been the de facto home for transgender issues for at least a decade.'[42] But 'home' is also a loaded word when thinking about a project to expand LGB to LGBT or LGBTI. Home suggests a *private* domain that provides a shelter from public scrutiny, but LGB people did not experience home as such until *Lawrence*, as cases such as *Bottoms* make clear. Home seems to construct natural affections and even a 'family resemblance' among L, G, B, T, and I people. However, as LGBTI people so often find out, homes are more varied, and family ties more precarious, and requiring of more active construction than any naturalistic fantasy implied by such taxonomies of people might imply. *Homelessness* is a problem that disproportionately affects LGBT youth and it remains 'open season' on intersex kids, who struggle along whilst their experiences receive very little by way of psychologists' recognition. Homes are also traditionally spaces where people – such as fathers – exercise proprietary rights over others, making marriage a dubious aim for LGBT psychology, and making the notion that adults are naturally best placed to act 'in the best interests of the children' for whom they care dangerous. Of all the many ways in which identities can be made invisible, spectacle, different, abnormal, or creative, I conclude that the distinction between adults and children continues to be the primary thing that limits the project of lesbian and gay-affirmative psychology from transforming psychology as a whole.

I think that to do justice to the intertwined histories of sexual minority adults, and particularly intersex and gender non-conforming children, it will be necessary to revisit some of lesbian and gay psychology's foundational moves, including the impulse to limit Queteletian normalization of lesbian and gay adults by psychiatry, but in way that allows our Galtonian fantasies about future generations to be unaffected by our recognition that it's great to be different. To be sure, even since the 2009 Report, events have moved forward.[43] During the writing of this book, the Centre for Addiction in Mental Health in Toronto, Canada, was closed and Kenneth Zucker removed as its director. Around the time of the Report's publication, I was critical of the trope of 'coming of age' which characterized some of the celebratory history of lesbian and gay-affirmative psychology of the 1990s.[44] I remain concerned that coming of age celebrates the termination of childhood in ways that defer questions about the rights of those who are children, and in so doing sets up a dynamic of disempowerment by which some adults are described as more childlike than others to the extent that they fit the norms that mental health professionals recognize. As the 2009 Report makes clear, the recognition that children are stigmatized does not automatically translate into actions that undo the stigmatized identity rather than the stigma itself.

Conclusions: the problems of the present

I want to conclude this book by asking my fellow historians of psychology to do better in the coming era in placing LGBT psychology at the center of our understanding of what psychology has been. Calls to understand social psychology's project as limited by historical context in the early 1970s took no account of the events described in Chapter 2.[45] In the early 1990s, historians of psychology asked bolder social constructionist questions about the nature, unity, and existence of the 'individual' and the 'subject' of psychological knowledge.[46] Historians of psychology were slow in noticing why sexuality was central to Foucault's argument that 'the human' had a historical ontology.[47] Several historians of psychology followed philosopher Ian Hacking's argument that psychology is a human science because 'looping effects' make scientists' representations of humans affect how humans act. However, the most developed attempt to apply Hacking's scheme to sexuality has needed to qualify this logic, and in ways that Hacking has himself critiqued.[48] As Pettit and Rutherford recently noted, LGBTI voices remain lacking in the history of psychology.[49] Without them, historians bear particular responsibility to consider how heteronormativity and the shortcomings of the 2009 APA Report might anchor understandings of what Thomas Teo calls *epistemological violence.*[50]

As such, I hope that this book has confirmed that lesbian and gay psychology is not an unimportant topic in the history of psychology. People who hunger for affirmation of transgender and intersex lives are not crazy to look to the recent history of lesbian and gay psychology as a historical analogy for success (despite what their doctors might tell them). It requires increasingly effortful exercise of the will to deny this field's centrality in psychology's recent history. To put this argument differently, consider the following questions: What's the best example of successful de-pathologization in the twentieth century? Which social groups were most affected when HIV/AIDS transformed what we understand enlightenment knowledge to be? Which issues have defined the relationship between psychology and the law in recent decades? What discovery made us feel that neuroscience might be a politically progressive narrative in the decade of the brain? Which central aspects of ourselves were most transformed by internet-mediated communication? What movement now grounds our understanding of affirmation that we did not have 40 years ago? Given the risks of living in the present, can American psychologists afford an ignorance of the recent history of LGBT psychology?

Notes

1 Meyerowitz (2004 [1980]).
2 Hale (n.d.), Rubin (1998).
3 Denny (1999), Bornstein (1994).
4 Parlee (1996).
5 Bailey (2003), Dreger (2015), Hegarty et al. (2004).
6 Tee & Hegarty (2006).
7 American Psychological Association (2009).
8 American Psychological Association (2009).
9 American Psychological Association (2009, p. 11).
10 American Psychological Association (2009, p. 18).
11 American Psychological Association (2009, p. 25).
12 American Psychological Association (2009, p. 7).
13 American Psychological Association (2009, p. 27).

14 McKenna & Kessler (2000, p. 67).
15 American Psychological Association (2009, p. 37).
16 See Stone (1992), American Psychological Association (2009, p. 295).
17 See Serano (2007), Ansara & Hegarty (2012).
18 American Psychological Association (2009, p. 26).
19 American Psychological Association (2009, p. 26).
20 American Psychological Association (2009, p. 44).
21 Ansara & Hegarty (2012).
22 American Psychological Association (2009, p. 26).
23 American Psychological Association (2009, p. 40)
24 American Psychological Association (2009, pp. 41–42).
25 American Psychological Association (2009, p. 49).
26 Lombardi et al. (2001).
27 American Psychological Association (2009, p. 43).
28 American Psychological Association (2009, p. 58).
29 American Psychological Assocation (2009, p. 46).
30 Egan & Perry (2001).
31 American Psychological Association (2009, p. 50).
32 Hill et al. (2005).
33 Stout et al. (2010), Ogilvie et al. (2006), Lundberg et al. (2017).
34 Jordan-Young (2012).
35 On ISNA's activism see Chase (1998), Davis (2015). See also Fausto-Sterling (1993) and Kessler (1990) on the status of Money's paradigm prior to the 1990s, Colapinto (2001) on the case of fraud, Diamond & Sigmundson (1997) on the call for a moratorium, and Preves (2003) on intersex-identity. See also Downing, Morland, & Sullivan (2015) for an insightful reading of John Money's work.
36 American Psychological Association (2009, p. 8).
37 Davis (2015, p. 70).
38 Sandberg, Callens, & Wisniewksi (2015).
39 See e.g., Cornwall (2013), Davis (2015), Feder (2014), Holmes (2009), Liao & Roen (2014).
40 Karkazis (2008).
41 American Psychological Association (2009, p. 5).
42 American Psychological Association (2009, p. 18).
43 Tosh (2015).
44 Hegarty (2009b).
45 Gergen (1973).
46 Danziger (1990).
47 Elsewhere I have discussed the divergence between sexuality scholars and historians of psychology and critical psychologists' discussions of Foucault (Hegarty, 2013).
48 See Hacking (1995, 2002), Stein (1999).
49 Rutherford & Pettit (2015).
50 Teo (2010).

References

Adelman, M. (1977). A comparison of professionally employed lesbians and heterosexual women on the MMPI. *Archives of Sexual Behavior*, 6, 193–201.

Ader, D. N., & Johnson, S. B. (1994). Sample description, reporting, and analysis of sex in psychological research: A look at APA and APA division journals in 1990. *American Psychologist*, 49, 216–218.

Aguero, J. E., Bloch, L., & Byrne, D. (1984). The relationships among sexual beliefs, attitudes, experience, and homophobia. *Journal of Homosexuality*, 10, 95–107.

Allport, G. W. (1954). *The nature of prejudice*. London: Addison-Wesley.

Altemeyer, B. (2001). Changes in attitudes toward homosexuals. *Journal of Homosexuality*, 42, 63–75.

American Psychiatric Association (1974). Position statement on homosexuality and civil rights. *American Journal of Psychiatry*, 131, 497.

American Psychiatric Association (1991). Position statement: Homosexuality and the immigration and naturalization service. *American Journal of Psychiatry*, 148, 1625.

American Psychological Association (2007). APA Task Force on the Sexualization of Girls. *Report of the APA Task Force on the sexualization of girls*. Downloaded May 3, 2017 from: www.apa.org/pi/women/programs/girls/report-full.pdf

American Psychological Association (2009). *Report of the American Psychological Association task force on gender identity and gender variance*. Washington, DC: American Psychological Association.

Anderson, C. A., Krull, D. S., & Weiner, B. (1996). Explanations: Processes and consequences. In E.T. Higgins and A.W. Kruglanski (Eds.), *Social psychology: Handbook of basic principles* (pp. 271–296). New York: Guilford.

Anderson, C. W., & Adley, A. R. (1997). *Gay and lesbian issues: Abstracts of the psychological and behavioral literature, 1985–1996*. Washington, DC: American Psychological Association.

Ansara, Y. G., & Hegarty, P. (2012). Cisgenderism in psychology: Pathologising and misgendering children from 1999 to 2008. *Psychology & Sexuality*, 3, 137–160.

Ansara, Y. G., & Hegarty, P. (2014). Methodologies of misgendering: Recommendations for reducing cisgenderism in psychological research. *Feminism & Psychology*, 24(2), 259–270.

Attwood, F. (2006). Sexed up: Theorizing the sexualization of culture. *Sexualities*, 9, 77–94.

Bachelor, W. F. (1984). AIDS. *American Psychologist*, 39, 1277–1278.

Bailey, J. M., Bobrow, D., Wolfe, M., & Mikach, S. (1995). Sexual orientation of adult sons of gay fathers. *Developmental Psychology*, 31, 124–129.

Bailey, J. M., & Pillard, R. C. (1991). A genetic study of male sexual orientation. *Archives of General Psychiatry*, 48, 1089–1096.

Bailey, J. M., & Zucker, K. J. (1995). Childhood sex-typed behavior and sexual orientation: A conceptual analysis and quantitative review. *Developmental Psychology*, 31, 43–55.

Bailey, M. (2003). *The man who would be queen: The science of gender-bending and transsexualism.* Washington, DC: Joseph Henry Press.

Balsam, K. F., Beauchaine, T. P., Rothblum, E. D., & Solomon, S. E. (2008). Three-year follow-up of same-sex couples who had civil unions in Vermont, same-sex couples not in civil unions, and heterosexual married couples. *Developmental Psychology*, 44, 102–116.

Barber, M. E. (2007). An interview with Nanette Gartrell, MD. In J. Drescher & J. P. Merlino (Eds.), *American psychiatry and homosexuality: An oral history* (pp. 131–144). New York: Routledge.

Barker, M. (2007). Heteronormativity and the exclusion of bisexuality in psychology. In V. Clarke & E. Peel (Eds.), *Out in psychology: Lesbian, gay, bisexual, trans, and queer perspectives* (pp. 86–118). Chichester, UK: Wiley.

Bartos, S. E., Berger, I., & Hegarty, P. (2014). Interventions to reduce sexual prejudice: A study space analysis and meta-analytic review. *Journal of Sex Research*, 51, 363–382.

Baum, A., & Nesselhof, S. E. (1988). Psychological research and the prevention, etiology, and treatment of AIDS. *American Psychologist*, 43, 900–906.

Baumeister, R. F. (2000). Gender differences in erotic plasticity: The female sex drive as socially flexible and responsive. *Psychological Bulletin*, 126, 347–374.

Baumrind, D. (1995). Commentary on sexual orientation: Research and social policy implications. *Developmental Psychology*, 31, 130–136.

Baunach, D. M. (2011). Decomposing trends in attitudes toward gay marriage, 1988–2006. *Social Science Quarterly*, 92, 346–363.

Baunach, D. M. (2012). Changing same-sex marriage attitudes in America from 1988 through 2010. *Public Opinion Quarterly*, 76, 364–378.

Bayer, R. (1981). *Homosexuality and American psychiatry: The politics of diagnosis.* Princeton, NJ: Princeton University Press.

Becker, A. B., & Scheufele, D. A. (2011). New voters, new outlook? Predispositions, social networks, and the changing politics of gay civil rights. *Social Science Quarterly*, 92, 324–345.

Belenky, M. F., Clinchy, B. M., Goldberger, N. R., & Tarule, J. M. (1986). *Women's ways of knowing: The development of self, voice, and mind.* New York: Basic Books.

Belkin, A., & Bateman, G. (Eds.) (2003). *Don't ask, don't tell: Debating the gay ban in the military.* Boulder, CO: Lynne Rienner.

Bell, A. P., Weinberg, M. S., & Hammersmith, S. K. (1981). *Sexual preference: Its development in men and women.* Bloomington: Indiana University Press.

Bem, S. L. (1974). The measurement of psychological androgyny. *Journal of Consulting and Clinical Psychology*, 42, 155–162.

Bem, S. L. (1993). *The lenses of gender: Transforming the debate on sexual inequality.* New Haven, CT: Yale University Press.

Bem, S. L. (1995). Dismantling gender polarization and compulsory heterosexuality: Should we turn the volume down or up? *The Journal of Sex Research*, 32, 329–334.

Bem, D. J. (1996). Exotic becomes erotic: A developmental theory of sexual orientation. *Psychological Review*, 103, 320–335.

Benjamin, L. T., Jr., & Crouse, E. M. (2002). The American Psychological Association's response to Brown v. Board of Education: The case of Kenneth B. Clark. *American Psychologist*, 57, 38–50.

Berkowitz, R., & Callen, M. (1997 [1982]). We know who we are: Two gay men declare war on promiscuity. In M. Blasius & S. Phelan (Eds.), *We are everywhere: A historical sourcebook of gay and lesbian politics* (pp. 563–571). New York: Routledge.

Berridge, V. (2011). Contemporary history of medicine and health. In M. Jackson (Ed.), *The Oxford handbook of the history of medicine* (pp. 117–132). Oxford: Oxford University Press.

Berrill, K. T. (1989). Anti-gay violence and victimization in the United States: An overview. *Journal of Interpersonal Violence*, 5, 274–294.

Bern, D. J. (1996). Exotic becomes erotic: A developmental theory of sexual orientation. *Psychological Review*, 103, 320–335.

Bersoff, D. N., & Ogden, D. W. (1991). APA amicus curiae briefs: Furthering lesbian and gay male civil rights. *American Psychologist*, 46, 950–956.

Berube, A. (1990). *Coming out under fire: The history of gay men and women in World War Two*. New York: Simon & Schuster.

Black, K., & Stevenson, M. (1984). The relationship of self-reported sex-role characteristics and attitudes toward homosexuality. *Journal of Homosexuality*, 10, 83–93.

Blackwood, E. (1985). Breaking the mirror: The construction of lesbianism and the anthropological discourse on homosexuality. *Journal of Homosexuality*, 11, 1–17.

Blumstein, P. W., & Schwartz, P. (1976). Bisexuality in women. *Archives of Sexual Behavior*, 5, 171–181.

Blumstein, P. W., & Schwartz, P. (1977). Bisexuality: Some social psychological issues. *Journal of Social Issues*, 33, 30–45.

Blumstein, P. W., & Schwartz, P. (1983). *American couples: Money, work, sex*. New York: William Morrow & Co.

Bolin, A. (1988). *In search of Eve: Transsexual rites of passage*. South Hadley, MA: Bergin & Harvey.

Bornstein, K. (1994). *Gender outlaw: On men, women and the rest of us*. New York: Routledge.

Boykin, K. (2005). *Beyond the down low: Sex, lies, and denial in Black America*. New York: Carroll & Graf Publishers.

Boysen, G., & Vogel, D. (2007). Biased assimilation and attitude polarization in response to learning about biological explanations of homosexuality. *Sex Roles*, 57, 755–762.

Bramel, D. A. (1963). Selection of a target for defensive projection. *Journal of Abnormal and Social Psychology*, 66, 318–324.

Brewer, P. R., & Wilcox, C. (2005). The polls – Trends. Same-sex marriage and civil unions. *Public Opinion Quarterly*, 69, 599–616.

Brown, L. S. (1989). New voices, new visions: Toward a lesbian/gay paradigm for psychology. *Psychology of Women Quarterly*, 13, 445–458.

Brown, L. S. (1992). While waiting for the revolution: The case for a lesbian feminist psychotherapy. *Feminism & Psychology*, 2, 239–253.

Brown, L. (2006, February 4). Interview by W. Pickren and A. Rutherford [Video recording]. Psychology's feminist voices oral history and online archive project. San Antonio, TX.

Bryant, K. (2006). Making gender identity disorder of childhood: Historical lessons for contemporary debates. *Sexuality Research & Social Policy*, 3, 23–39.

Buckley, W. F. (1986). Crucial steps in combating the AIDS epidemic: Identify all the carriers. *New York Times*, March 18, p. A27.

Buechel, C., & Hegarty, P. (2007). Modern prejudice at work: Effects of homonegativity and perceived erotic value of lesbians and gay men on heterosexuals' reactions to explicit and discrete couples. *Lesbian & Gay Psychology Review*, 8, 71–82.

Buhrke, R. A., Ben-Ezra, L. A., Hurley, M. E., & Ruprecht, L. J. (1992). Content analysis and methodological critique of articles concerning lesbian and gay male issues in counseling journals. *Journal of Counseling Psychology*, 39, 91–99.

Burke, P. (1996). *Gender shock: Exploding the myths of male and female*. New York: Anchor Books.

Burks, D. J. (2011). Lesbian, gay, and bisexual victimization in the military: An unintended consequence of 'Don't Ask, Don't Tell'? *American Psychologist*, 66, 604–613.

Burman, E. (2008). *Deconstructing developmental psychology*, 2nd ed. New York: Routledge.

Butler, J. (1990). *Gender trouble: Feminism and the subversion of identity*. New York: Routledge.

Butler, J. (1991). Imitation and gender insubordination. In D. Fuss (Ed.), *Inside/out: Lesbian theories, gay theories* (pp. 13–31). New York: Routledge.

Butler, J. (1993). *Bodies that matter: On the discursive limits of 'sex'*. New York: Routledge.

Cabaj, R. P., & Purcell, D. W. (1998). *On the road to same-sex marriage: A supportive guide to psychological, political, and legal issues*. San Francisco, CA: Jossey-Bass.

Cahill, S. (2005). Welfare moms and the two grooms: The concurrent promotion and restriction of marriage in US public policy. *Sexualities*, 8, 169–187.

Callen, M., & Berkowitz, R. (1997 [1983]). How to have sex in an epidemic. In M. Blasius & S. Phelan (Eds.), *We are everywhere: A historical sourcebook of gay and lesbian politics* (pp. 571–574). New York: Routledge.

Cameron, P., & Cameron, K. (1997). Did the APA misrepresent the scientific literature to courts in support of homosexual custody? *The Journal of Psychology: Interdisciplinary and Applied*, 131, 313–332.

Carver, P. R., Egan, S. K., & Perry, D. G. (2004). Children who question their heterosexuality. *Developmental Psychology*, 40, 43–53.

Cass, V. (1979). Homosexual identity formation: A theoretical model. *Journal of Homosexuality*, 4, 219–235.

Cass, V. (1996). Sexual orientation identity formation: A Western phenomenon. In R. P. Cabaj & T. S. Stein (Eds.), *Textbook of homosexuality and mental health* (pp. 227–251). Arlington, VA: American Psychiatric Association.

Cautin, R. L. (2009). The founding of the Association for Psychological Science: Part 1. Dialectical tensions within organized psychology. *Perspectives on Psychological Science*, 4, 211–223.

Chase, C. (1998). Hermaphrodites with attitude: Mapping the emergence of intersex political activism. *GLQ*, 4, 189–211.

Cherlin, A. (2004). The deinstitutionalization of American marriage. *Journal of Marriage and Family*, 66, 848–861.

Chivers, M. L., Rieger, G., Latty, E., & Bailey, J. M. (2004). A sex difference in the specificity of sexual arousal. *Psychological Science*, 15, 736–744.

Chodorow, N. J. (1978). *The reproduction of mothering: Psychoanalysis and the sociology of gender*. Berkeley: University of California Press.

Cianiotto, J., & Cahill, S. (2005). *Youth in the crosshairs: The third wave of ex-gay activism*. Washington, DC: National Gay and Lesbian Task Force Policy Institute. Downloaded May 3, 2017 from: www.thetaskforce.org/static_html/downloads/reports/reports/You thInTheCrosshairs.pdf

Clark, K. B., Chein, I., & Cook, S. W. (2004). The effects of segregation and the consequences of desegregation: A (September 1952) social science statement in the Brown v. Board of Education of Topeka Supreme Court case. *American Psychologist*, 59, 495–501.

Clarke, V. (2000). 'Stereotype, attack and stigmatize those who disagree': Employing scientific rhetoric in debates about lesbian and gay parenting. *Feminism & Psychology*, 10, 152–159.

Coates, T. J., Stall, R. D., Kegeles, S. M., Lo, B., Morin, S. F., & McKusick, L. (1988). AIDS antibody testing: Will it stop the AIDS epidemic? Will it help people infected with HIV? *American Psychologist*, 43, 859–864.

Coates, T. J., Temoshok, L., & Mandel, J. (1984). Psychosocial research is essential to understanding and treating AIDS. *American Psychologist*, 39, 1309–1314.

Cohen, C. (1997a). *The boundaries of Blackness: AIDS and the breakdown of Black politics.* Chicago, IL: University of Chicago Press.

Cohen, C. (1997b). Punks, bulldaggers and welfare queens: The radical potential of queer politics? *GLQ: A Journal of Gay and Lesbian Studies,* 3, 437–465.

Colapinto, J. (2001). *As nature made him: The boy who was raised as a girl.* New York: Harper Perennial.

Committee on Lesbian and Gay Concerns (1991). Avoiding heterosexual bias in language. *American Psychologist,* 46, 973–974.

Conger, J. J. (1975). Proceedings of the American Psychological Association, Incorporated, for the year 1974: Minutes of the annual meeting of the Council of Representatives. *American Psychologist,* 30, 620–651.

Connolly, C. (1996). An analysis of judicial opinions in same-sex visitation and adoption cases. *Behavioral Sciences & the Law,* 14, 187–203.

Connolly, C. (1998). The description of gay and lesbian families in second-parent adoption cases. *Behavioral Sciences & the Law,* 16, 225–236.

Conrad, P., & Markens, S. (2001). Constructing the 'gay gene' in the news: Optimism and skepticism in the American and British press. *Health,* 5, 373–400.

Constantinople, A. (1973). Masculinity–femininity. An exception to a famous dictum? *Psychological Bulletin,* 80, 398–407.

Cornwall, S. (2013). *Sex and uncertainty in the body of Christ; Intersex conditions and Christian theology.* London: Routledge.

Corrigan, P. W., River, L. P., Lundin, R. K., Penn, D. L., Uphoff-Wasowski, K., Campion, J. et al. (2001). Three strategies for changing attributions about severe mental illness. *Schizophrenia Bulletin,* 27, 187–195.

Crandall, C. S. (1994). Prejudice against fat people: Ideology and self-interest. *Journal of Personality and Social Psychology,* 66, 882–894.

Crandall, C. S., & Eshleman, A. (2003). A justification-suppression model of the expression and experience of prejudice. *Psychological Bulletin,* 129, 414–446.

Crandall, C. S., Eshleman, A., & O'Brien, L. (2002). Social norms and the expression and suppression of prejudice: The struggle for internalization. *Journal of Personality and Social Psychology,* 82, 359–378.

Crimp, D. (1987). How to have promiscuity in an epidemic. *October,* 43, 35.

Crocker, J., & Major, B. (1989). Social stigma and self-esteem: The self-protective properties of stigma. *Psychological Review,* 96, 608–630.

Cross, W. E. (1971). The negro-to-black conversion experience. *Black World,* 20(9), 13–27.

Cross, W. E. (1991). *Shades of black: Diversity in African-American identity.* Philadelphia, PA: Temple University Press.

Cuenot, R. G., & Fugita, S. S. (1982). Perceived homosexuality: Measuring heterosexual attitudinal and nonverbal reactions. *Personality and Social Psychology Bulletin,* 8, 100–106.

Curtin, N., Hegarty, P., & Stewart, A. J. (2012). Expanding the research community in LGBT psychology: Collaborative studies from the international institute. *Psychology and Sexuality,* 3, 187–194.

Danziger, K. (1990). *Constructing the subject: Historical origins of psychological research.* Cambridge: Cambridge University Press.

Danziger, K. (2006). Universalism and indigenization in the history of modern psychology. In A. C. Brock (Ed.), *Internationalizing the history of psychology* (pp. 208–225). New York: New York University Press.

D'Augelli, A. R., & Hershberger, S. L. (1993). Lesbian, gay, and bisexual youth in community settings: Personal challenges and mental health problems. *American Journal of Community Psychology*, 21, 421–448.

Davis, G. (2015). *Contesting intersex: The dubious diagnosis*. New York: New York University Press.

Davis, J. A., & Smith, T. W. (1992). *The NORC General Social Survey: A user's guide*. Thousand Oaks, CA: Sage Publications.

Davison, G. C. (1976). Homosexuality: The ethical challenge. *Journal of Consulting and Clinical Psychology*, 44, 157–162.

Davison, G. C., & Wilson, G. T. (1973). Attitudes of behavior therapists toward homosexuality. *Behavior Therapy*, 4, 686–696.

Defense of Marriage Act, The (DOMA) (1996). (Pub.L. 104–199), 110 Stat. 241.

DeLamater, J. D., & Hyde, J. S. (1998). Essentialism v. social constructionism in the study of human sexuality. *Journal of Sex Research*, 35, 10–18.

Denny, D. (1999). Transgender in the United States: A brief discussion. *SIECUS Report*, 28, 8–13.

Des Jarlais, D. C., & Friedman, S. R. (1988). The psychology of preventing AIDS among intravenous drug users: A social learning conceptualization. *American Psychologist*, 43, 865–870.

Desjarlais, R. (1994). Struggling along: The possibilities for experience among the homeless mentally ill. *American Anthropologist*, 96, 886–901.

Diamond, L. M. (1998). Development of sexual orientation among adolescent and young adult women. *Developmental Psychology*, 34, 1085–1095.

Diamond, L. M. (2003). What does sexual orientation orient? A biobehavioral model distinguishing romantic love and sexual desire. *Psychological Review*, 110, 173–192.

Diamond, L. M. (2005). 'I'm straight, but I kissed a girl': The trouble with American media representations of female–female sexuality. *Feminism & Psychology*, 15, 104–110.

Diamond, L. M. (2008a). Female bisexuality from adolescence to adulthood: Results from a 10-year longitudinal study. *Developmental Psychology*, 44, 5–14.

Diamond, L. M. (2008b). *Sexual fluidity: Understanding women's love and desire*. Cambridge, MA: Harvard University Press.

Diamond, L. M. (2011, August 6). Interview by L. Granek [Video Recording]. Psychology's feminist voices oral history and online archive project. Washington, DC.

Diamond, L., & Rosky, C. J. (2016). Scrutinizing immutability: Research on sexual orientation and U.S. legal advocacy for sexual minorities. *Journal of Sex Research*, 53, 363–391.

Diamond, M., & Sigmundson, K. (1997). Management of intersexuality: Guidelines for dealing with persons with ambiguous genitalia. *Archives of Pediatric and Adolescent Medicine*, 151, 1046–1050.

Dooley, P. A. (1995). Perceptions of the onset of controllability of AIDS and helping judgments: An attributional analysis. *Journal of Applied Social Psychology*, 25, 858–869.

Dorner, G. (1976). *Hormones and brain differentiation*. Amsterdam, Netherlands: Elsevier.

Downing, L., Morland, I., & Sullivan, N. (2014). *Fuckology: Critical essays on John Money's diagnostic concepts*. Chicago: University of Chicago Press.

Dreger, A. (2015). *Galileo's middle finger: Heretics, activists, and the search for justice in science*. New York: Penguin.

Drescher, J. (1998). I'm your handyman: A history of reparative therapies. *Journal of Homosexuality*, 36, 19–42.

Drescher, J. (2006). The Spitzer study and the culture wars. In J. Drescher & K. J. Zucker (Eds.), *Ex-gay research: Analyzing the Spitzer study and its relation to science, religion, politics, and culture* (pp. 107–112). Binghamton, NY: Harrington Park Press/The Haworth Press.

Driver-Linn, E. (2003). Where is psychology going? Structural fault lines revealed by psychologists' use of Kuhn. *American Psychologist*, 58, 269–278.

Duggan, L. (2003). *The twilight of equality: Neoliberalism, cultural politics and the attack on democracy.* Boston, MA: Beacon Press.

Egan, P. J., & Sherill, K. (2009). *California's Propostion 8: What happened and what does the future hold?* New York: National Gay and Lesbian Task Force Policy Institute.

Egan, S. K., & Perry, D. G. (2001). Gender identity: A multidimensional analysis with implications for psychosocial adjustment. *Developmental Psychology*, 37, 451–463.

Epstein, D., Kehily, M. J., & Reynold, E. (2012). Culture, policy and the un/marked child: Fragments of the sexualization debates. *Gender & Education*, 24, 249–254.

Epstein, S. (1996). *Impure science, AIDS, activism, and the politics of knowledge.* Berkeley: University of California Press.

Epstein, S. (2007). *Inclusion: The politics of difference in medical research.* Chicago, IL: University of Chicago Press.

Erikson, E. H. (1959). Identity and the life cycle: Selected papers. *Psychological Issues*, 1, 1–171.

Erikson, E. H. (1964). *Childhood and society*, 2nd ed. Oxford: W. W. Norton.

Erzen, T. (2006). *Straight to Jesus: Sexual and Christian conversions in the ex-gay movement.* Berkeley: University of California Press.

Eskridge, W. N. Jr. (2002). *Gaylaw: Challenging the apartheid of the closet.* Cambridge, MA: Harvard University Press.

Evans, A., Riley, S., & Shankar, A. (2010). Technologies of sexiness: Theorizing women's engagement in the sexualization of culture. *Feminism & Psychology*, 20, 114–131.

Faderman, L. (1991). *Odd girls and twilight lovers: A history of lesbian life in twentieth century America.* New York: Columbia University Press.

Fahs, B. (2009). Compulsory bisexuality?: The challenges of modern sexual fluidity. *Journal of Bisexuality*, 9, 431–449.

Falbo, T., & Peplau, L. A. (1980). Power strategies in intimate relationships. *Journal of Personality and Social Psychology*, 38, 618–628.

Falk, P. J. (1989). Lesbian mothers: psychosocial assumptions in family law. *American Psychologist*, 44, 941–947.

Falomir-Pichastor, J. M., & Hegarty, P. (2014). Maintaining distinctions under threat: Heterosexual men endorse the biological theory of sexuality when equality is the norm. *British Journal of Social Psychology*, 53, 731–751.

Falomir-Pichastor, J. M., & Mugny, G. (2009). 'I'm not gay … I'm a real man!': Heterosexual men's gender self-esteem and sexual prejudice. *Personality and Social Psychology Bulletin*, 35, 1233–1243.

Fausto-Sterling, A. (1992). *Myths of gender*, 2nd ed. New York: Basic Books.

Fausto-Sterling, A. (1993). The five sexes. *The Sciences* (March/April), 20–25.

Feder, E. (2014). *Making sense of intersex: Changing clinical perspectives in medicine.* Bloomington: Indiana University Press.

Fee, E., & Fox, D. M. (Eds.) (1988). *AIDS: The burdens of history.* Berkeley: University of California Press.

Ferrara, A. J. (1984). My personal experience with AIDS. *American Psychologist*, 39, 1285–1287.

Fine, M., & Asch, A. (1988). Disability beyond stigma: Social interaction, discrimination, and activism. *Journal of Social Issues*, 44, 3–21.

Finlay, S.-J., Clarke, V., & Wilkinson, S. (2003). 'Marriage' special issues. *Feminism & Psychology*, 13(4), 411–414.

Finlay, W. M. L. (2005). Pathologizing dissent: Identity politics, Zionism and the 'self-hating Jew'. *British Journal of Social Psychology*, 44, 201–222.

Finlay, W. M. L. (2007). The propaganda of extreme hostility: Denunciation and the regulation of the group. *British Journal of Social Psychology*, 46, 323–341.

Finnegan, D. G., & Cook, D. (1984). Special issues affecting the treatment of male and lesbian alcoholics. *Alcoholism Treatment Quarterly*, 1, 85–98.

Fischer, D.H. (1970). *Historian's fallacies: Toward a logic of historical thought*. New York: Harper Collins.

Fisher, K. (1983). Stress: The unseen killer in AIDS. *APA Monitor*, 14(7) (July), 1, 20–21.

Fort, J., Steiner, C. M., & Conrad, F. (1971). Attitudes of mental health professionals toward homosexuality and its treatment. *Psychological Reports*, 29, 347–350.

Foucault, M. (1978). *The history of sexuality* (Vol. 1), trans. Robert Hurley. New York: Random House.

Fox, R. E. (1992). Proceedings of the American Psychological Association, Incorporated, for the year 1991: Minutes of the annual meeting of the Council of Representatives. *American Psychologist*, 47, 893–934.

Freund, K., Nagler, E., Langevin, R., Zajac, A., & Steiner, B. (1974). Measuring feminine gender identity in homosexual males. *Archives of Sexual Behavior*, 3, 249–260.

Frias-Navarro, D., Monterde-i-Bort, H., Pascual-Soler, M., & Badenes-Ribera, L. (2015). Etiology of homosexuality and attitudes toward same-sex parenting: A randomized study. *Journal of Sex Research*, 52, 151–161.

Gannon, L., Luchetta, T., Rhodes, K., Pardie, L., & Segrist, D. (1992). Sex bias in psychological research. Progress or complacency? *American Psychologist*, 47, 389–396.

Garnets, L., Hancock, K. A., Cochran, S. D., Goodchilds, J., & Peplau, L. A. (1991). Issues in psychotherapy with lesbians and gay men: A survey of psychologists. *American Psychologist*, 46, 964–972.

Garnets, L., Herek, G. M., & Levy, B. (1992). Violence and victimization of lesbians and gay men: Mental health consequences. In G. M. Herek & K. T. Berrill (Eds.), *Hate crimes: Confronting violence against lesbians and gay men* (pp. 207–226). Thousand Oaks, CA: Sage Publications.

Gartrell, N., Kraemer, H., & Brodie, H. K. (1974). Psychiatrists' attitudes toward female homosexuality. *Journal of Nervous and Mental Disease*, 159, 141–144.

Gathorne-Hardy, J. (1998). *Sex the measure of all things: A life of Alfred C. Kinsey*. Bloomington: Indiana University Press.

Gentile, P., & Kinsman, G. (2000). Psychology, national security and the 'fruit machine'. *History and Philosophy of Psychology Bulletin*, 12, 18–24.

Gergen, K. J. (1973). Social psychology as history. *Journal of Personality and Social Psychology*, 26, 309–320.

Gideonse, T. (1997). Are we an endangered species? *The Advocate*, 734, 28–30.

Gill, R. (2009). Beyond the 'sexualization of culture' thesis: An intersectional analysis of 'sixpacks', 'midriffs' and 'hot lesbians' in advertising. *Sexualities*, 12, 137–160.

Gilligan, C. (1982). *In a different voice: Psychological theory and women's development*. Cambridge, MA: Harvard University Press.

Glenn, N. D., & Weaver, C. N. (1979). Attitudes toward premarital, extramarital and homosexual relations in the U.S. in the 1970s. *Journal of Sex Research*, 15, 108–118.

Goffman, E. (1963). *Stigma: Notes on the management of a spoiled identity*. New York: Simon & Schuster.

Golombok, S., Spencer, A., & Rutter, M. (1983). Children in lesbian and single-parent households: Psychosexual and psychiatric appraisal. *Child Psychology & Psychiatry & Allied Disciplines*, 24, 551–572.

Gonsierek, J. (1993). Foreword. In G. M. Herek & B. Greene (Eds.), *Lesbian and gay psychology: Theory, research and clinical applications. Psychological perspectives on lesbian and gay issues* (Vol. 1, p. vii). Thousand Oaks, CA: Sage.

Green, R. (1982). The best interests of the child with a lesbian mother. *Bulletin of the American Academy of Psychiatry & the Law*, 10, 7–15.

Green, R. (1987). *The sissy boy syndrome: The developmental of homosexuality*. New Haven, CT: Yale University Press.

Green, R. (1988). The immutability of (homo)sexual orientation: Behavioral science implications for a constitutional (legal) analysis. *Journal of Psychiatry & Law*, 16, 537–575.

Greene, B. (2009). The use and abuse of religious beliefs in dividing and conquering between socially marginalized groups: The same-sex marriage debate. *American Psychologist*, 64, 698–709.

Greene, B. (2009, September 11). Interview by L. Granek [Video Recording]. Psychology's feminist voices oral history and online archive project. New York. http://www.feministvoices.com/beverly-greene/

Greeno, C. G., & Maccoby, E. E. (1986). How different is the 'different voice'? *Signs*, 11, 310–316.

Grob, G. (1991). Origins of DSM-I: A study in appearance and reality. *American Journal of Psychiatry*, 148, 421–431.

Hacking, I. (1995). The looping effects of human kinds. In D. Sperber, D. Premack, & A. J. Premack (Eds.), *Causal cognition: A multi-disciplinary debate* (pp. 351–383). Oxford: Oxford University Press.

Hacking, I. (2002). How 'natural' are 'kinds' of sexual orientation? *Law and Philosophy*, 21, 95–107.

Haider-Markel, D. P., & Joslyn, M. R. (2008). Beliefs about the origins of homosexuality and support for gay rights: An empirical test of attribution theory. *Public Opinion Quarterly*, 72, 291–310.

Hald, G. M., Seaman, C., & Linz, D. (2014). Sexuality and pornography. In D. L. Tolman, L. M. Diamond, J. A. Bauermeister, W. H. George, J. G. Plaus, & L. M. Ward (Eds.), *APA handbook of sexuality and psychology, Vol. 2: Contextual approaches* (pp. 3–35). Washington, DC: American Psychological Association.

Hale, J. (n.d.). Suggested rules for non-transsexuals writing about transsexuals, transsexuality, transesexualism, or trans_____. Downloaded May 3, 2017 from: https://sandystone.com/hale.rules.html

Hall, N. R. (1988). The virology of AIDS. *American Psychologist*, 43, 907–913.

Halley, J. E. (1993). The construction of heterosexuality. In M. Warner (Ed.), *Fear of a queer planet* (pp. 82–102). Minneapolis: University of Minnesota Press.

Halley, J. E. (1994). Sexual orientation and the politics of biology: A critique of the argument from immutability. *Stanford Law Journal*, 36, 301–366.

Halperin, D. (1995). *Saint Foucault: Towards a gay hagiography*. New York: Oxford University Press.

Halperin, D. M. (2003). The normalization of queer theory. *Journal of Homosexuality*, 45, 339–343.

Hamer, D. H., Hu, S., Magnuson, V. L., Hu, N., & Pattatucci, A. M. (1993). A linkage between DNA markers on the X chromosome and male sexual orientation. *Science*, 261, 321–327.

Hammack, P. L., & Windell, E. P. (2011). Psychology and the politics of same-sex desire in the United States: An analysis of three cases. *History of Psychology*, 14, 220–248.

Hare-Mustin, R. T., & Marecek, J. (1990). *Making a difference: Psychology and the construction of gender*. New Haven, CT: Yale University Press.

Harvey, D. (1990). *The condition of postmodernity: An enquiry into the origins of cultural change.* Malden, MA: Blackwell.

Haslam, N., & Levy, S. R. (2006). Essentialist beliefs about homosexuality: Structure and implications for prejudice. *Personality and Social Psychology Bulletin,* 32, 471–485.

Haslam, N., Rothschild, L., & Ernst, D. (2002). Are essentialist beliefs associated with prejudice? *British Journal of Social Psychology,* 41, 87–100.

Hegarty, P. (1997). Materializing the hypothalamus: A performative account of the 'gay brain'. *Feminism & Psychology,* 7, 355–372.

Hegarty, P. (2001). 'Real science', deception experiments and the gender of my lab coat: Toward a new laboratory manual for lesbian and gay psychology. *International Journal of Critical Psychology,* 1(4), 91–108.

Hegarty, P. (2002). 'It's not a choice, it's the way we're built': Symbolic beliefs about sexual orientation in the United States and in Britain. *Journal of Community and Applied Social Psychology,* 12, 1–14.

Hegarty, P. (2003). Homosexual signs and heterosexual silences: Rorschach studies of male homosexuality from 1921 to 1967. *Journal of the History of Sexuality,* 12, 400–423.

Hegarty, P. (2006). Where's the sex in sexual prejudice? *Lesbian and Gay Psychology Review,* 7, 264–275.

Hegarty, P. (2007a). What comes after discourse analysis for LGBTQ psychology? In E. A. Peel and V. C. Clarke (Eds.) *Out in psychology: LGBTQ perspectives* (pp. 41–57). Chichester: Wiley and Sons.

Hegarty, P. (2007b). Getting dirty: Psychology's history of power. *History of Psychology,* 10, 75–91.

Hegarty, P. (2009a). Toward an LGBT-informed paradigm for children who break gender norms: Comment on Drummond et al. (2008) and Reiger et al. (2008). *Developmental Psychology,* 45, 895–900.

Hegarty, P. (2009b). Queerying lesbian and gay psychology's coming of age: Was history just kid stuff? In M. O'Rourke and N. Giffney (Eds.), *The Ashgate research companion to queer theory* (pp. 514–544). Aldershot, UK: Ashgate.

Hegarty, P. (2010). A stone in the soup? Changes in sexual prejudice and essentialist beliefs among British students in a class on LGBT psychology. *Psychology and Sexuality,* 1, 3–20.

Hegarty, P. (2013). *Gentlemen's disagreement: Alfred Kinsey, Lewis Tennan, and the sexual politics of smart men.* Chicago, IL: University of Chicago Press.

Hegarty, P., & Bruckmüller, S. (2013). Asymmetric explanations of group differences: Experimental evidence of Foucault's disciplinary power. *Social and Personality Psychology Compass,* 7, 176–186.

Hegarty, P., & Buechel, C. (2011). 'What blokes want lesbians to be': On FHM and the socialization of pro-lesbian attitudes among heterosexual-identified men. *Feminism & Psychology,* 21, 240–247.

Hegarty, P., & Golden, A. M. (2008). Attributions about the controllability of stigmatized traits: Antecedents or justifications of prejudice? *Journal of Applied Social Psychology,* 38, 1023–1044.

Hegarty, P., Lenihan, P., Barker, M., & Moon, L. (2004). The Bailey affair: Psychology perverted: A response. Downloaded May 3, 2017 from: www.tsroadmap.com/info/bailey-critique.html

Hegarty, P., & Massey, S. (2006). Anti-homosexual prejudice … as opposed to what? Queer theory and the social psychology of anti-homosexual attitudes. *Journal of Homosexuality,* 52, 47–71.

Hegarty, P., Parslow, O., Ansara, Y. G., & Quick, F. L. (2013). Androcentrism: Changing the landscape without levelling the playing field. In M. K. Ryan & N. R. Branscombe (Eds.), *The Sage Handbook of Gender and Psychology* (pp. 29–44). London: Sage.

Hegarty, P., & Pratto, F. (2001). The effects of social category norms and stereotypes on explanations for intergroup differences. *Journal of Personality and Social Psychology*, 80, 723–735.

Hegarty, P., & Pratto, F. (2004). The differences that norms make: Empiricism, social constructionism, and the interpretation of group differences. *Sex Roles*, 50, 445–453.

Henriques, J., Hollway, W., Urwin, C., Venn, C., & Walkerdine, V. (1984). *Changing the Subject. Psychology, Social Regulation and Subjectivity*. London: Methuen & Co.

Henry, P. J. (2008). College sophomores in the laboratory redux: Influences of a narrow data base on social psychology's view of the nature of prejudice. *Psychological Inquiry*, 19, 49–71.

Herek, G. M. (1984). Attitudes toward lesbians and gay men: A factor analytic study. *Journal of Homosexuality*, 10, 1–21.

Herek, G. M. (1986a). On heterosexual masculinity: Some psychical consequences of the social construction of gender and sexuality. *American Behavioral Scientist*, 29, 563–677.

Herek, G. M. (1986b). The instrumentality of attitudes: Toward a neofunctional theory. *Journal of Social Issues*, 42, 99–114.

Herek, G. M. (1987). Can functions be measured? A new perspective on the functional approach to attitudes. *Social Psychology Quarterly*, 50, 285–303.

Herek, G. M. (1989). Hate crimes against lesbians and gay men: Issues for research and policy. *American Psychologist*, 44, 948–955.

Herek, G. M. (1993). Sexual orientation and military service: A social science perspective. *American Psychologist*, 48, 538–549.

Herek, G. M. (1995). Preface. In G. M. Herek & B. Greene (Eds.), *AIDS, identity and community: The HIV epidemic and lesbians and gay men: Psychological perspectives on lesbian and gay issues, Volume 2*. Thousand Oaks, CA: Sage Publications.

Herek, G. M. (1998). Bad science in the service of stigma: A critique of the Cameron group's survey studies. In G. M. Herek (Ed.), *Stigma and sexual orientation: Understanding prejudice against lesbians, gay men, and bisexuals* (pp. 223–255). Thousand Oaks, CA: Sage Publications.

Herek, G. M. (2006). Evaluating interventions to alter sexual orientation: Methodological and ethical considerations. In J. Drescher, & K. J. Zucker (Eds.), *Ex-gay research: Analyzing the Spitzer study and its relation to science, religion, politics, and culture* (pp. 131–136). Binghamton, NY: Harrington Park Press/The Haworth Press.

Herek, G. M., & Berrill, K. T. (Eds.) (1992). *Hate crimes: Confronting violence against lesbians and gay men*. Thousand Oaks, CA: Sage.

Herek, G. M., & Capitanio, J. P. (1995). Black heterosexuals' attitudes toward lesbians and gay men in the United States. *Journal of Sex Research*, 32, 95–105.

Herek, G. M., Cogan, J. C., & Gillis, J. R. (2002). Victim experiences in hate crimes based on sexual orientation. *Journal of Social Issues*, 58, 319–339.

Herek, G. M., Gillis, J. R., & Cogan, J. C. (1999). Psychological sequelae of hate-crime victimization among lesbian, gay, and bisexual adults. *Journal of Consulting and Clinical Psychology*, 67, 945–951.

Herek, G., & Glunt, E. (1988). The epidemic of stigma. *American Psychologist*, 43, 886–891.

Herek, G. M., Kimmel, D. C., Amaro, H., & Melton, G. B. (1991). Avoiding heterosexual bias in psychological research. *American Psychologist*, 46, 957–963.

Herman, D. (1996). *The antigay agenda: Orthodox vision and the Christian right.* Chicago, IL: University of Chicago Press.

Herman, E. (1995). *The romance of American psychology: Political culture in the age of experts.* Berkeley: University of California Press.

Herman, E. (1996). All in the family: Lesbian motherhood meets popular psychology in a dysfunctional ear. In E. Lewin (Ed.), *Inventing lesbian cultures in America* (pp. 83–104). Boston, MA: Beacon Press.

Hershberger, S. L., & D'Augelli, A. R. (1995). The impact of victimization on the mental health and suicidality of lesbian, gay, and bisexual youths. *Developmental Psychology*, 31, 65–74.

Hershberger, S. L., Pilkington, N. W., & D'Augelli, A. R. (1997). Predictors of suicide attempts among gay, lesbian, and bisexual youth. *Journal of Adolescent Research*, 12, 477–497.

Hill, D. B., Rozanski, C., Carfagnini, J., & Willoughby, B. (2005). Gender identity disorders in childhood and adolescence: A critical inquiry. *Journal of Psychology & Human Sexuality*, 17, 7–34.

Hire, R. O. (2007). An interview with Frank Rundle, MD. In J. Drescher & J. P. Merlino (Eds.), *American psychiatry and homosexuality: An oral history* (pp. 115–130). New York: Routledge.

Holmes, M. (Ed.) (2009). *Critical intersex.* Abingdon, UK: Routledge.

Hooker, E. (1957). The adjustment of the male overt homosexual. *Journal of Projective Techniques*, 21, 18–31.

Hooker, E. (1958). Male homosexuality in the Rorschach. *Journal of Projective Techniques & Personality Assessment*, 22, 33–54.

Hooker, E. (1993). Reflections of a 40-year exploration: A scientific view on sexuality. *American Psychologist*, 48, 450–453.

Hubbard, K., & Hegarty, P. (2014). Why is the history of heterosexuality essential? Beliefs about the history of sexuality and their relationship to sexual prejudice. *Journal of Homosexuality*, 61, 471–490.

Hubbard, K., & Hegarty, P. (2016). Blots and all: A history of the Rorschach ink blot test in Britain. *Journal of the History of the Behavioral Sciences*, 52, 146–166.

Hubbard, R., & Wald, E. (1993). *Exploding the gene myth: How genetic information is produced and manipulated by scientists, physicians, employers, insurance companies, educators, and law enforcers.* Boston, MA: Beacon Press.

Hunter, J. (2007). Remembering Emery Hetrick, MD. In J. Drescher & J. P. Merlino (Eds.), *American psychiatry and homosexuality: An oral history* (pp. 179–192). New York: Routledge.

Hyde, J. S. (1984). Children's understanding of sexist language. *Developmental Psychology*, 20, 697–706.

Icard, L. D. (1986). Black gay men and conflicting social identities: Sexual orientation versus racial identity. *Journal of Social Work & Human Sexuality*, 4, 83–93.

Jagose, A. (1996). *Queer theory: An introduction.* New York: New York University Press.

Jetten, J., Spears, R., & Postmes, T. (2004). Intergroup distinctiveness and differentiation: A meta-analytic integration. *Journal of Personality and Social Psychology*, 86, 862–879.

Johnson, K. (2015). *Sexuality: A psychosocial manifesto.* Cambridge: Polity Press.

Jones, J. (1997). *Alfred Kinsey: A public/private life.* New York: W. W. Norton.

Jordan-Young, R. M. (2012). Hormones, context, and 'Brain Gender': A review of evidence from congenital adrenal hyperplasia. *Social Science & Medicine*, 74, 1738–1744.

Joseph, J. G., Emmons, C.-A., Kessler, R. C., Wortman, C. B., O'Brien, K., Hocker, W. T., & Schaefer, C. (1984). Coping with the threat of AIDS: An approach to psychosocial assessment. *American Psychologist*, 39, 1297–1302.

Kameny, F. (1997 [1965]). Does research into homosexuality matter? In M. Blasius & S. Phelan (Eds.), *We are everywhere: A historical sourcebook of gay and lesbian politics* (pp. 335–339). New York: Routledge.

Kameny, F. (2009). How it all started. *Journal of Gay & Lesbian Mental Health*, 13, 76–81.

Karkazis, K. (2008). *Fixing sex: Intersex, medical authority and lived experience.* Durham, NC: Duke University Press.

Kessler, S. (1990). The medical construction of gender: Case management of intersexed infants. *Signs: Journal of Women in Culture and Society*, 16, 3–26.

Kessler, S., & McKenna, W. (1978). *Gender: An ethnomethodological approach.* Chicago, IL: University of Chicago Press.

Kiecolt-Glaser, J. K., & Glaser, R. (1988). Psychological influences on immunity: Implications for AIDS. *American Psychologist*, 43, 892–898.

Kimmel, D. C., & Browning, C. (1999). A history of Division 44 (Society for the Psychological Study of Lesbian, Gay, and Bisexual Issues). In D. A. Dewsbury (Ed.), *Unification through division: Histories of the divisions of the American Psychological Association, Vol. IV* (pp. 129–150). Washington, DC: American Psychological Association.

King, M., Semlyen, J., Tai, S. S., Killaspy, H., Osborn, D., Popelyuk, D., & Nazareth, I. (2008). A systematic review of mental disorder, suicide, and deliberate self harm in lesbian, gay and bisexual people. *BMC Psychiatry*, 8, 70–86.

Kippax, S., & Race, K. (2003). Sustaining safe practice: 20 years on. *Social Science and Medicine*, 57, 1–12.

Kirkpatrick, M., Smith, C., & Roy, R. (1981). Lesbian mothers and their children: A comparative survey. *American Journal of Orthopsychiatry*, 5, 545–551.

Kitzinger, C. (1987). *The social construction of lesbianism.* London: Sage.

Kitzinger, C. (1994). Should psychologists study sex differences? *Feminism & Psychology*, 4, 501–506.

Kitzinger, C., & Coyle, A. (2002). Introducing lesbian and gay psychology. In A. Coyle & C. Kitzinger (Eds.), *Lesbian and gay psychology: New perspectives* (pp. 1–29). Malden, UK: Blackwell.

Kitzinger, C., & Perkins, R. (1993). *Changing our minds: Lesbian feminism and psychology.* New York: New York University Press.

Kitzinger, C., & Wilkinson, S. (1994). Virgins and queers: Rehabilitating heterosexuality? *Gender & Society*, 8, 444–462.

Kitzinger, C., & Wilkinson, S. (1995). Transitions from heterosexuality to lesbianism: the discursive production of lesbian identities. *Developmental Psychology*, 31, 95–104.

Kitzinger, C., & Wilkinson, S. (2004). Social advocacy for equal marriage: The politics of 'rights' and the psychology of 'mental health'. *Analyses of Social Issues and Public Policy*, 4, 173–194.

Kitzinger, C., & Wilkinson, S. (2015, May 26). Interview with J. Young [Video Recording]. Psychology's feminist voices oral history and online archive project. York, UK.

Kitzinger, C., Wilkinson, S., & Perkins, R. (1992). Theorizing heterosexuality. *Feminism & Psychology*, 2(3), 293–324.

Klein, F. (1979). *The bisexual option: A concept of one hundred percent intimacy.* Gettysburg, PA: Arbor House.

Koop, C. E. (1986). *The Surgeon General's report on Acquired Immune Deficiency Syndrome.* Washington, DC: United States Public Health Service.

Kramer, L. (2005 [1983]). 1,112 and counting. In I. Morland & A. Willox (Eds.), *Queer theory* (pp. 28–39). Basingstoke, UK: Palgrave.

Kuhn, T. S. (1970). *The structure of scientific revolutions.* Chicago, IL: University of Chicago Press.

Kurdek, L. A. (1993). The allocation of household labor in gay, lesbian, and heterosexual married couples. *Journal of Social Issues*, 49, 127–139.

Kurdek, L. A. (2005). What do we know about gay and lesbian couples? *Current Directions in Psychological Science*, 14(5), 251–254.

Lancaster, R. N. (2003). *The trouble with nature: Sex in science and popular culture*. Berkeley: University of California Press.

Landén, M., & Innala, S. (2002). The effect of a biological explanation on attitudes towards homosexual persons. A Swedish national sample study. *Nordic Journal of Psychiatry*, 56, 181–186.

Lannutti, P. J. (2005). For better or worse: Exploring the meanings of same-sex marriage within the lesbian, gay, bisexual and transgendered community. *Journal of Social and Personal Relationships*, 22, 5–18.

Laumann, E. O., Gagnon, J. H., Michael, R. T., & Michaels, S. (1994). *The social organization of sexuality*. Chicago, IL: University of Chicago Press.

Lee, I. C., & Crawford, M. (2007). Lesbians and bisexual women in the eyes of scientific psychology. *Feminism & Psychology*, 17, 109–127.

LeVay, S. (1991). A difference in hypothalamic structure between heterosexual and homosexual men. *Science*, 253, 1034–1037.

Levitt, E. E., & Klassen, A. D. (1974). Public attitudes toward homosexuality: Part of the 1970 National Survey by the Institute for Sex Research. *Journal of Homosexuality*, 1, 29–43.

Lewin, E. (1993). *Lesbian mothers: Accounts of gender in American society*. Ithaca, NY: Cornell University Press.

Lewin, E. (1999). *Recognizing ourselves*. New York: Columbia University Press.

Lewin, M. (1984a). 'Rather worse than folly?' Psychology measures femininity and masculinity, 1. In M. Lewin (Ed.), *In the shadow of the past: Psychology portrays the sexes* (pp. 135–178). New York: Columbia University Press.

Lewin, M. (1984b). Psychology measures femininity and masculinity, 2: From '13 gay men' to the instrumental-expressive distinction. In M. Lewin (Ed.), *In the shadow of the past: Psychology portrays the sexes* (pp. 179–204). New York: Columbia University Press.

Lewis, G. B. (2003). Black–White differences in attitudes toward homosexuality and civil rights. *Public Opinion Quarterly*, 67, 20.

Lewis, G. B. (2009). Does believing homosexuality is innate increase support for gay rights? *Policy Studies Journal*, 37, 669–693.

Liao, L.-M., & Roen, K. (Eds.) (2014). Intersex/DSD post-Chicago: New developments and challenges for psychologists. *Psychology & Sexuality*, 5(1). Published online.

Linz, D., Donnerstein, E., & Penrod, S. (1987). The findings and recommendations of the Attorney General's Commission on Pornography: Do the psychological 'facts' fit the political fury? *American Psychologist*, 42, 946–953.

Loftus, J. (2001). America's liberalization in attitudes toward homosexuality, 1973–1998. *American Sociological Review*, 66, 762–782.

Loiacano, D. K. (1989). Gay identity issues among Black Americans: Racism, homophobia, and the need for validation. *Journal of Counseling & Development*, 68, 21–25.

Lombardi, E. L., Wilchins, R. A., Priesing, D., & Malouf, D. (2001). Gender violence: Transgender experiences with violence and discrimination. *Journal of Homosexuality*, 42, 89–101.

Lorde, A. (1984). *Sister outsider: Essays and speeches*. Trumansburg, NY: Crossing Press.

Louderback, L. A., & Whitley, B. E., Jr. (1997). Perceived erotic value of homosexuality and sex-role attitudes as mediators of sex differences in heterosexual college students' attitudes toward lesbians and gay men. *Journal of Sex Research*, 34, 175–182.

Lourea, D. N. (1985). Psychosocial issues related to counseling bisexuals. *Journal of Homosexuality*, 11, 51–62.

Lundberg, T., Lindström, A., Roen, K., & Hegarty, P. (2017). From knowing nothing to knowing now: Parents' experiences of caring for their children with Congenital Adrenal Hyperplasia. *Journal of Pediatric Psychology* 42, 520–529.

Maher, M. J., Landini, K., Emano, D. M., Knight, A. M., Lantz, G. D., Parrie, M., & Sever, L. M. (2009). Hirschfeld to Hooker to Herek to high schools: A study of the history and development of GLBT empirical research, institutional policies, and the relationship between the two. *Journal of Homosexuality*, 56, 921–958.

Malyon, A. K. (1982). Psychotherapeutic implications of internalized homophobia in gay men. *Journal of Homosexuality*, 7, 59–69.

Martin, E. (1994). *Flexible bodies: Tracking immunity in American culture from the days of polio to the age of AIDS*. Boston, MA: Beacon Press.

Martin, J. L., & Vance, C. S. (1984). Behavioral and psychosocial factors in AIDS: Methodological and substantive issues. *American Psychologist*, 39, 1303–1308.

Matarazzo, J. D., Bailey, W. A., Kraut, A. G., & Jones, J. M. (1988). APA and AIDS: The evolution of a scientific and professional initiative in the public interest. *American Psychologist*, 43, 978–982.

Mays, V. M., & Cochran, S. D. (1988). Issues in the perception of AIDS risk and risk reduction activities by Black and Hispanic/Latina women. *American Psychologist*, 43, 949–957.

McConahay, J. B. (1983). Modern racism and modern discrimination: The effects of race, racial attitudes, and context on simulated hiring decisions. *Personality and Social Psychology Bulletin*, 9, 551–558.

McConaghy, N., Proctor, D., & Barr, R. (1972). Subjective and penile plethysmography responses to aversion therapy for homosexuality: A partial replication. *Archives of Sexual Behavior*, 2, 65–78.

McKenna, K. Y. A., & Bargh, J. A. (1998). Coming out in the age of the Internet: Identity 'demarginalization' through virtual group participation. *Journal of Personality and Social Psychology*, 75, 681–694.

McKenna, W., & Kessler, S. J. (2000). Retrospective response. *Feminism & Psychology*, 10, 66–72.

McNemar, Q. (1946). Opinion-attitude methodology. *Psychological Bulletin*, 43, 289–374.

Meara, N. M., & Myers, R. A. (1999). A history of Division 17 (Counseling Psychology): Establishing stability amid change. In D. A. Dewsbury (Ed.), *Unification through division: Histories of the divisions of the American Psychological Association, Vol. 3* (pp. 9–41). Washington, DC: American Psychological Association.

Medin, D. M. (1989). Concepts and conceptual structure. *American Psychologist*, 44, 1469–1481.

Mednick, M. T. (1989). On the politics of psychological constructs: Stop the bandwagon, I want to get off. *American Psychologist*, 44, 1118–1123.

Melton, G. B. (1988). Ethical and legal issues in AIDS-related practice. *American Psychologist*, 43, 941–947.

Messing, A. E., Schoenberg, R., & Stephens, R. K. (1984). Confronting homophobia in health care settings: Guidelines for social work practice. *Journal of Social Work & Human Sexuality*, 2, 65–74.

Meyer, I. H. (1995). Minority stress and mental health in gay men. *Journal of Health and Social Behavior*, 36, 38–56.

Meyer, I. H. (2003). Prejudice, social stress, and mental health in lesbian, gay, and bisexual populations: Conceptual issues and research evidence. *Psychological Bulletin*, 129, 674–697.

Meyer-Bahlburg, H. F. L. (1977). Sex hormones and male homosexuality in comparative perspective. *Archives of Sexual Behavior*, 6, 297–325.

Meyerowitz, J. (2004 [1980]). *How sex changed: A history of transsexuality in the United States.* Cambridge, MA: Harvard University Press.

Milgram, S. (1974). *Obedience to authority.* New York: Harper Perennial.

Miller, D. T., Taylor, B., & Buck, M. L. (1991). Gender gaps: Who needs to be explained? *Journal of Personality and Social Psychology, 61*, 5–12.

Miller, K. P. (2008). Essentialist beliefs about homosexuality, attitudes toward gay men and lesbians, and religiosity: Change within a structure of interconnected beliefs. Unpublished dissertation: Ohio State University.

Millett, G., Malebranche, D., Mason, B., & Spikes, P. (2005). Focusing 'down low': Bisexual Black men, HIV risk and heterosexual transmission. *Journal of the National Medical Association*, 97, 52s–59s.

Minton, H. L. (1997). Queer theory: Historical roots and implications for psychology. *Theory & Psychology, 7*, 337–353.

Minton, H. L. (2002). *Departing from deviance: A history of homosexual rights and emancipatory science in America.* Chicago, IL: University of Chicago Press.

Mitchell, R. W., & Dezarn, L. (2014). Does knowing why someone is gay influence tolerance? Genetic, environmental, choice, and 'reparative' explanations. *Sexuality & Culture: An Interdisciplinary Quarterly, 18*, 994–1009.

Money, J., & Ehrhardt, A. A. (1971). Fetal hormones and the brain: Effect on sexual dimorphism of behavior – A review. *Archives of Sexual Behavior*, 1, 214–262.

Morin, S. F. (1974). Educational programs as a means of changing attitudes toward gay people. *Homosexual Counseling Journal, 1*, 160–165.

Morin, S. F. (1977). Heterosexual bias in psychological research on lesbianism and male homosexuality. *American Psychologist, 32*, 629–637.

Morin, S. F. (1984). AIDS in one city: An interview with Mervyn Silverman, Director of Health, San Francisco. *American Psychologist, 39*, 1294–1296.

Morin, S. F. (1988). AIDS: The challenge to psychology. *American Psychologist, 43*, 838–842.

Morin, S. F., Charles, K. A., & Malyon, A. K. (1984). The psychological impact of AIDS on gay men. *American Psychologist, 39*, 1288–1293.

Morin, S. F., & Rothblum, E. D. (1991). Removing the stigma: Fifteen years of progress. *American Psychologist, 46*, 947–949.

Morin, S. F. & Schultz, S. J. (1978). The gay movement and the rights of children. *Journal of Social Issues*, 34, 137–148.

Morrison, M. A., & Morrison, T. G. (2002). Development and validation of a scale measuring modern prejudice toward gay men and lesbian women. *Journal of Homosexuality, 43*, 15–37.

Morton, T. A., & Postmes, T. (2009). When differences become essential: Minority essentialism in response to majority treatment. *Personality and Social Psychology Bulletin, 35*, 656–668.

Mosher, D. L., & O'Grady, K. E. (1979). Homosexual threat, negative attitudes toward masturbation, sex guilt, and males' sexual and affective reactions to explicit sexual films. *Journal of Consulting and Clinical Psychology, 47*, 860–873.

Mucciaroni, G., & Killian, M. L. (2004). Immutability, science and legislative debate over gay, lesbian and bisexual rights. *Journal of Homosexuality*, 47, 53–77.

Mustanski, B. S., Chivers, M. L., & Bailey, J. M. (2002). A critical review of recent biological research on human sexual orientation. *Annual Review of Sex Research, 13*, 89–140.

Nicolosi, J. (2006). Finally, recognition of a long-neglected population. In J. Drescher & K. J. Zucker (Eds.), *Ex-gay research: Analyzing the Spitzer study and its relation to science, religion, politics, and culture* (pp. 159–163). Binghamton, NY: Harrington Park Press/The Haworth Press.

NIHM Task Force on Homosexuality (1972). Final Report of the Task Force on Homosexuality. Chevy Chase, MD: National Institute of Mental Health.

O'Connor, C., & Joffe, H. (2013). How has neuroscience affected lay understandings of personhood? A review of the evidence. *Public Understanding of Science, 22*, 15.

Ogilvie, C. M., Crouch, N. S., Rumsby, G., Creighton, S. M., Liao, L., & Conway, G. S. (2006). Congenital adrenal hyperplasia in adults: A review of medical, surgical and psychological issues. *Clinical Endocrinology, 64*, 2–11.

Oldham, J. D., & Kasser, T. (1999). Attitude change in response to information that male homosexuality has a biological basis. *Journal of Sex and Marital Therapy, 25*, 121–124.

Olson, L. R., Cadge, W., & Harrison, J. T. (2006). Religion and public opinion about same-sex marriage. *Social Science Quarterly, 87*, 340–360.

Ordover, N. (1996). Eugenics, the gay gene, and the science of backlash. *Socialist Review, 26*, 125–144.

Parker, R., di Mauro, D., Filiano, B., Garcia, J., Muñoz-Laboy, M., & Sember, R. (2004). Global transformations and intimate relations in the 21st century: Social science research on sexuality and the emergence of sexual health and sexual rights frameworks. *Annual Review of Sex Research, 15*, 362–398

Parlee, M. (1996). Situated knowledges of personal embodiment: Transgender activists' and psychological theorists' perspectives on 'sex' and 'gender'. *Theory & Psychology, 6*, 625–645.

Pateman, C. (1988). *The sexual contract.* Cambridge: Polity Press.

Patterson, C. J. (1992). Children of lesbian and gay parents. *Child Development, 63*, 1025–1042.

Patterson, C. J. (1995). Sexual orientation and human development: An overview. *Developmental Psychology, 31*, 3–11.

Patterson, C. (2006). Children of lesbian and gay parents. *Current Directions in Psychological Science, 15*, 241–244.

Pearl, M. L., & Galupo, M. P. (2007). Development and validation of the attitudes toward same-sex marriage scale. *Journal of Homosexuality, 53*, 117–134.

Peplau, L. A., Garnets, L. D., Spalding, L. R., Conley, T. D., & Veniegas, R. C. (1998). A critique of Bem's 'Exotic Becomes Erotic' theory of sexual orientation. *Psychological Review, 105*, 387–394.

Perkins, R. E. (1991). Therapy for lesbians? The case against. *Feminism & Psychology, 1*, 325–338.

Pershing, S. B. (1994). 'Entreat me not to leave thee.' Bottoms v Bottoms and the custody rights of gay and lesbian parents. *William and Mary Bill of Rights Journal, 3*, 289–325.

Peterson, J. L., & Marín, G. (1988). Issues in the prevention of AIDS among Black and Hispanic men. *American Psychologist, 43*, 871–877.

Pettigrew, T. F., & Tropp, L. R. (2006). A meta-analytic test of intergroup contact theory. *Journal of Personality and Social Psychology, 90*, 751–783.

Pettit, M. (2011). The SPSSI task force on sexual orientation, the nature of sex, and the contours of activist science. *Journal of Social Issues, 67*, 92–105.

Pettit, M., & Hegarty, P. (2014). Psychology and sexuality in historical time. In D. L. Tolman, L. M. Diamond, J. A. Bauermeister, W. H. George, J. G. Pfaus, L. M. Ward (Eds.), *APA handbook of sexuality and psychology, Vol. 1: Person-based approaches* (pp. 63–78). Washington, DC: American Psychological Association.

Phillips, D., Fischer, S. C., & Groves, G. A. (1976). Alternative behavioral approaches to the treatment of homosexuality. *Archives of Sexual Behavior, 5*, 223–228.

Picketty, T. (2014). Capital in the twenty-first century, trans. A. Goldhammer. Cambridge, MA: Harvard University Press.

Pickren, W. E., & Schneider, S. F. (2005). *Psychology and the National Institute of Mental Health: A historical analysis of science, practice and policy*. Washington, DC: American Psychological Association.

Pickren, W. E., & Tomes, H. (2002). The legacy of Kenneth B. Clark to the APA: The Board of Social and Ethical Responsibility for Psychology. *American Psychologist, 57*, 51–59.

Piliavin, I. M., Rodin, J., & Piliavin, J. A. (1969). Good Samaritanism: An underground phenomenon? *Journal of Personality and Social Psychology, 13*, 289–299.

Piskur, J., & Degelman, D. (1992). Effect of reading a summary of research about biological bases of homosexual orientation on attitudes toward homosexuals. *Psychological Reports, 71*, 1219–1225.

Pope, M. (2012). First we were sane, now we are legal: The historic position of Division 44 in LGBT civil rights. *Division 44 Newsletter, 28*(8), 14–21.

Pratarelli, M. E., & Donaldson, J. S. (1997). Immediate effects of written material on attitudes toward homosexuality. *Psychological Reports, 81*, 1411–1415.

Presidential Commission on the Human Immunodeficiency Virus Epidemic (1988). *Report of the Presidential Commission on the HIV Epidemic*, 0-214-701:QE3. Washington, DC: U.S. Government Printing Office.

Preves, S. (2003). *Intersex and identity: The contested self*. New Brunswick, NJ: Rutgers University Press.

Pruitt, M. V. (2002). Size matters: A comparison of anti- and progay organizations' estimates of the size of the gay population. *Journal of Homosexuality, 42*, 21–29.

Raja, S., & Stokes, J. P. (1998). Assessing attitudes toward lesbians and gay men: The Modern Homophobia Scale. *Journal of Gay, Lesbian, & Bisexual Identity, 3*, 113–134.

Reimer, N. K., Kok, G., & Hospers, H. J. (2014). Prejudice and the 'gay gene': The implications of genetic essentialism for sexual prejudice and gay stereotype. Unpublished manuscript: Oxford University. https://www.researchgate.net/publication/266020699_Prejudice_and_the_'gay_gene'_The_implications_of_genetic_essentialism_for_sexual_prejudice_and_gay_stereotype_endorsement

Reinisch, J. M. (1974). Fetal hormones, the brain and human sex differences: A hueristic, integrative review of the recent literature. *Archives of Sexual Behavior, 3*, 51–90.

Reinisch, J. M., Sanders, S. A., & Ziemba-Davis, M. (1988). The study of sexual behavior in relation to the transmission of human immunodeficiency virus: Caveats and recommendations. *American Psychologist, 43*, 921–927.

Reizenstein, R. (1986). A structural equation analysis of Weiner's attribution-affect model of helping behavior. *Journal of Personality and Social Psychology, 50*, 1123–1133.

Rekers, G. A. (1978). Comment: A priori values and research on homosexuality. *American Psychologist, 33*, 510–512.

Rekers, G. A., & Lovaas, O. I. (1974). Behavioral treatment of deviant sex-role behaviors in a male child. *Journal of Applied Behavior Analysis, 7*, 173–190.

Rich, A. (1980). Compulsory heterosexuality and lesbian existence. *Signs: Journal of Women in Culture and Society, 5*, 631–660.

Rieger, G., Chivers, M. L., & Bailey, J. M. (2005). Sexual arousal patterns of bisexual men. *Psychological Science, 16*, 579–584.

Riger, S. (1992). Epistemological debates, feminist voices: Science, social values, and the study of women. *American Psychologist, 47*, 730–740.

Riggle, E. D. B., Rostosky, S. S., & Horne, S. G. (2009). Marriage amendments and lesbian, gay, and bisexual individuals in the 2006 election. *Sexuality Research & Social Policy: A Journal of the NSRC, 6*, 80–89.

Rind, B. (2006). Sexual orientation change and informed consent in reparative therapy. In J. Drescher & K. J. Zucker (Eds.), *Ex-gay research: Analyzing the Spitzer study and its relation to science, religion, politics, and culture* (pp. 165–170). Binghamton, NY: Harrington Park Press/The Haworth Press.

Rivers, D. (2010). 'In the best interests of the child': lesbian and gay parenting custody cases, 1967–1985. *Journal of Social History*, 43, 917–943.

Rogers, C. R. (1961). *On becoming a person*. Oxford: Houghton Mifflin.

Rosario, M., Rotheram-Borus, M. J., & Reid, H. (1996). Gay-related stress and its correlates among gay and bisexual male adolescents of predominantly Black and Hispanic background. *Journal of Community Psychology*, 24, 136–159.

Rosario, V. A. (Ed.) (1997). *Science and homosexualities*. New York: Routledge.

Rose, N., & Abi-Rached, J. M. (2013). *Neuro: The new brain sciences and the management of the mind*. Princeton, NJ: Princeton University Press.

Ross, M. W. (1980). Retrospective distortion in homosexual research. *Archives of Sexual Behavior*, 9, 523–531.

Ross, M. W. (2005). Typing, doing, and being: Sexuality and the internet. *Journal of Sex Research*, 42, 342–352.

Rostosky, S. S., Riggle, E. D. B., Gray, B. E., & Hatton, R. L. (2007). Minority stress experiences in committed same-sex couple relationships. *Professional Psychology: Research and Practice*, 38, 392–400.

Rothblum, E. D. (1988). Introduction: Lesbianism as a model of a positive lifestyle for women. *Women & Therapy*, 8, 1–12.

Rothblum, E. (2009, March 14). Interview by T. Beaulieu, A. Karera, & J. MacKay. [Video Recording]. Psychology's feminist voices oral history and online archive project. Newport, RI. http://www.feministvoices.com/esther-rothblum/

Rotheram-Borus, M. J., Hunter, J., & Rosario, M. (1994). Suicidal behavior and gay-related stress among gay and bisexual male adolescents. *Journal of Adolescent Research*, 9, 498–508.

Rubin, H. S. (1998). Phenomenology as method in trans studies. *GLQ: A Journal of Lesbian and Gay Studies*, 4, 263–281.

Ruck, N. (2016). Controversies on evolutionism: On the construction of scientific boundaries in public and internal scientific controversies about evolutionary psychology and sociobiology. *Theory & Psychology*, 26, 691–705.

Rutherford, A. (2009). *Beyond the box: B. F. Skinner's technology of behavior from laboratory to life, 1950s to 1970s*. Toronto, ON: University of Toronto Press.

Rutherford, A., & Pettit, M. (2015). Feminism and/in/as psychology: The public sciences of sex and gender. *History of Psychology*, 18, 223–237.

Sandberg, D. E., Callens, N., & Wisniewksi, A. B. (2015). Disorders of sex development (DSD): Networking and standardization considerations. *Hormones and Metabolism Research*, 47, 387–393.

Savin-Williams, R. C. (1989). Coming out to parents and self-esteem among gay and lesbian youths. *Journal of Homosexuality*, 18, 1–35.

Savin-Williams, R. C., & Ream, G. L. (2003). Suicide attempts among sexual-minority male youth. *Journal of Clinical Child and Adolescent Psychology*, 32(4), 509–522.

Schmalz, J. (1993). Poll finds an even split on homosexuality's cause. *New York Times*, March 15, p. A14.

Schmitt, M. T., Lehmiller, J. J., & Walsh, A. L. (2007). The role of heterosexual identity threat in differential support for same-sex 'civil unions' versus 'marriages'. *Group Processes & Intergroup Relations*, 10, 443–455.

Schneider, W., & Lewis, I. A. (1984). The straight story on homosexuality and gay rights. *Public Opinion*, 7 (February/March), 16–20, 59–60.

Scott, J. W. (1991). The evidence of experience. *Critical Inquiry*, 17, 773–797.

Sears, D. O. (1986). College sophomores in the laboratory: Influences of a narrow data base on social psychology's view of human nature. *Journal of Personality and Social Psychology, 51,* 515–530.

Sedgwick, E. K. (1990). *Epistemology of the closet.* Berkeley: University of California Press.

Sedgwick, E. K. (1991). How to bring your kids up gay. *Social Text, 91,* 18–27.

Sedgwick, E. K. (1997). Paranoid reading and reparative reading, or you're so paranoid you probably think this introduction is about you. In E. K. Sedgwick (Ed.), *Novel gazing: Queer readings in fiction.* Durham, NC: Duke University Press.

Senaro, J. (2007). *Whipping girl: A transsexual woman on sexism and the scapegoating of femininity.* Berkeley, CA: Seal Press.

Shapin, S. (1995). *A social history of truth: Civility and science in seventeenth century England.* Chicago, IL: University of Chicago Press.

Sheldon, J. P., Pfeffer, C. A., Jayaratne, T. E., Feldbaum, M., & Petty, E. M. (2007). Beliefs about the etiology of homosexuality and about the ramifications of discovering its possible genetic origin. *Journal of Homosexuality, 52,* 11–150.

Sherkat, D. E., de Vries, K. M., & Creek, S. (2010). Race, religion, and opposition to same-sex marriage. *Social Science Quarterly, 91,* 80–98.

Shidlo, A., & Schroeder, M. (2002). Changing sexual orientation: A consumers' report. *Professional Psychology: Research and Practice, 33,* 249–259.

Shilts, R. (1987). *And the band played on.* New York: Penguin.

Singer, E., Rogers, T. F., & Corcoran, M. (1987). A report: AIDS. *Public Opinion Quarterly, 51,* 580–595.

Soule, S. (2004). Going to the chapel? Same-sex marriage bans in the United States. *Social Problems,* 51, 453–477.

Smith, K. T. (1971). Homophobia: A tentative personality profile. *Psychological Reports, 29,* 1091–1094.

Snyder, K. (2006). *The G quotient: Why gay executives are excelling as leaders … and what every manager needs to know.* San Francisco, CA: John Wiley & Sons.

Spitzer, R. L. (2003). Can some gay men and lesbians change their sexual orientation? 200 participants reporting a change from homosexual to heterosexual orientation. *Archives of Sexual Behavior, 32,* 403–417.

Spitzer, R. L. (2012). Spitzer reassesses his 2003 study of reparative therapy of homosexuality. *Archives of Sexual Behavior, 41,* 757–757.

Stacey, J., & Biblarz, T. J. (2001). (How) does sexual orientation of parents matter? *American Sociological Review, 65,* 159–183.

Stall, R., Coates, T. J., & Hoff, C. (1988). Behavioral risk reduction for HIV infection among gay and bisexual men: A review of results from the United States. *American Psychologist, 43,* 878–885.

Stein, E. (1999). *The mismeasure of desire: The science, theory and ethics of sexual orientation.* Oxford: Oxford University Press.

Stone, S. (1992). The empire strikes back: A post-transsexual manifesto. *Camera Obscura, 10,* 150–176.

Storms, M. D. (1979). Sex role identity and its relationships to sex role attributes and sex role stereotypes. *Journal of Personality and Social Psychology, 37,* 1779–1789.

Stout, S. A., Litvak, M., Robbins, N. M., & Sandberg, D. E. (2010). Congenital adrenal hyperplasia: Classification of studies employing psychological endpoints. *International Journal of Pediatric Endocrinology,* Article ID: 191520.

Sullivan, A. (1996). Virtually normal: An argument about homosexuality. New York: Vintage Books.

Silvestre, A. J. (1999). Gay male, lesbian and bisexual health-related research funded by the National Institutes of Health between 1974 and 1992. *Journal of Homosexuality, 37,* 81–94.

Taylor, L. D. (2005). All for him: Articles about sex in American lad magazines. *Sex Roles, 52,* 153–163.

Tee, N., & Hegarty, P. (2006). Predicting opposition to the civil rights of trans persons in the United Kingdom. *Journal of Community & Applied Social Psychology, 16*(1), 70–80.

Teo, T. (2010). What is epistemological violence in the empirical social sciences? *Social and Personality Psychology Compass, 4,* 295–303.

Terry, J. (1997). The seductive power of science in the making of deviant subjectivity. In V. A. Rosario (Ed.), *Science and homosexualities* (pp. 271–289). New York: Routledge.

Terry, J. (1999). *An American obsession: Science, medicine and homosexuality in American society.* Chicago, IL: University of Chicago Press.

Tiefer, L. (2001). A new view of women's sexual problems: Why new? Why now? *Journal of Sex Research, 38,* 89–96.

Tiefer, L. (2005, October, 31). Interview by L. Granek. [Video Recording]. Psychology's feminist voices oral history and online archive project. Toronto, ON, Canada.

Tosh, J. (2015). *Perverse psychology: The pathologization of sexual violence and transgenderism.* New York: Routledge.

Treas, J. (2002). How cohorts, education and ideology all shaped a new sexual revolution on American attitudes toward nonmarital sex, 1972–1998. *Sociological Perspectives, 45,* 267–283.

Treichler, P. A. (1987). AIDS, homophobia and biomedical discourse: An epidemic of signification. *October, 43,* 31–70.

Tribe, L. H. (2004). Lawrence v. Texas: The fundamental right that dare not speak its name. *Harvard Law Review, 17,* 1893–1955.

Turner, W. (2000). *A genealogy of queer theory.* Philadelphia, PA: Temple University Press.

Vandiver, B. J., Cross, W. E., Jr., Worrell, F. C., & Fhagen-Smith, P. E. (2002). Validating the Cross Racial Identity Scale. *Journal of Counseling Psychology, 49,* 71–85.

Van Vooris, R., & Wagner, M. (2002). Among the missing: Content on lesbian and gay people in social work journals. *Social Work, 47,* 345–354.

Veniegas, R. C., & Conley, T. D. (2000). Biological research on women's sexual orientations: Evaluating the scientific evidence. *Journal of Social Issues, 56,* 267–282.

Voeller, B., David, P. M., Stephanie, A. S., & June Machover, R. (1990). Some uses and abuses of the Kinsey scale. In D. P. McWhirter, S. A. Sanders, & J. M. Reinisch (Eds.), *Homosexuality/heterosexuality: Concepts of sexual orientation* (pp. 32–38). New York: Oxford University Press.

Walster, E., Walster, G. W., & Berscheid, E. (1978). *Equity: Theory and research.* Boston, MA: Allyn and Bacon.

Warner, M. (1993). Introduction. In M. Warner (Ed.), *Fear of a queer planet* (pp. vii–xxxi). Minneapolis: University of Minnesota Press.

Warner, M. (1999). *The trouble with normal: Sex, politics and the ethics of queer life.* New York: Free Press.

Warner, N. (2004). Towards a queer research methodology. *Qualitative Research in Psychology, 1,* 321–337.

Waterman, A. D., Reid, J. D., Garfield, L. D., & Hoy, S. J. (2001). From curiosity to care: Heterosexual student interest in sexual diversity courses. *Teaching of Psychology, 28,* 21–26.

Watkins, J. D. (1988). Responding to the HIV epidemic: A national strategy. *American Psychologist, 43,* 849–851.

Watters, A. T. (1986). Heterosexual bias in psychological research on lesbianism and male homosexuality (1979–1983), utilizing the bibliographic and taxonomic system of Morin (1977). *Journal of Homosexuality, 13*, 35–58.

Weinberg, G. (1972). *Society and the healthy homosexual.* Oxford: Anchor.

Weiner, B. (1993). On sin versus sickness: A theory of perceived responsibility and social motivation. *American Psychologist, 48*, 957–965.

Weiner, B., Perry, R. P., & Magnusson, J. (1988). An attributional analysis of reactions to stigmas. *Journal of Personality and Social Psychology*, 55, 738–748.

Weinrich, J. D. (1995). Biological research on sexual orientation: A critique of the critics. *Journal of Homosexuality, 28*, 197–213.

Weisstein, N. (1971). Psychology constructs the female: or the fantasy life of the male psychologist (with some of the fantasies of his friends, the male biologist and the male anthropologist). *Social Education, 35*, 362–373.

Wetherell, M. (1997). Linguistics repertoires and literary criticism. New directions for a social psychology of gender. In M. M. Gergen & S. N. Davis (Eds.), *Toward a new psychology of gender* (pp. 149–167). New York: Routledge.

Whitley, B. E. (1990). The relationship of heterosexuals' attributions for the causes of homosexuality to attitudes towards lesbians and gay men. *Personality and Social Psychology Bulletin, 16*, 369–377.

Wilkinson, S. (n.d.) History of the psychology of sexualities. Downloaded November 1, 2016 from: www.bps.org.uk/networks-and-communities/member-microsite/psychology-sexualities-section/history-psychology-sexualities

Wittig, M. (1992). *The straight mind and other essays.* Boston, MA: Beacon Press.

Worrell, F. C., Cross, W. E., Jr., & Vandiver, B. J. (2001). Nigrescence theory: Current status and challenges for the future. *Journal of Multicultural Counseling and Development, 29*, 201–213.

Yang, A. S. (1997). The polls – trends: Attitudes toward homosexuality. *Public Opinion Quarterly, 61*, 477–507.

Yep, G. A., Lovaas, K. E., & Elia, J. P. (2003). A critical appraisal of assimilationist and radical ideologies underlying same-sex marriage in LGBT communities in the United States. *Journal of Homosexuality, 45*, 45–64.

Zucker, K. J., & Spitzer, R. L. (2005). Was the Gender Identity Disorder of Childhood diagnosis introduced into DSM-III as a backdoor maneuver to replace homosexuality? A historical note. *Journal of Sex & Marital Therapy, 31*, 31–42.

Names Index

Subject Index

Adjustment, psychological: 3, 52–55. *see also* self-esteem.
Advocate, The: 69
AIDS/HIV, 4, 26–35; activism, 31, 51, 96; African-Americans and 27–28, 33, 78, n87 f63; AZT as treatment for, 30–3; contact tracing, 45; gay related immune deficiency (GRID) as designation of AIDS, 27; high risk groups, 27, 34; HIV tests, 30; impact on same-sex couples, 59; IV drug users, 32; psychological research on, 28–29, 32–35; theories of causes of AIDS, 28–29; National Academy of Sciences Report, 31; Presidential Commission (1987), 31–32; sodomy laws and HIV/AIDS, 45; transformations in knowledge demanded by epidemic, 26, 30–31.
American Association for Behavior Therapists, 20
American Civil Liberties Union (ACLU), 45
American Medical Association, 7
American Psychiatric Association, 1, 7–8, 10, 47–48, 77
American Psychological Association, 1, 5, 77; amicus briefs on sexual orientation, 48–64; Board for the Advancement of Psychology in the Public Interest, 9; Board of Social and Ethical Responsibility in Psychology (BSERP), 9, 10, 28, 29–30; Committee on Women, 19; Committee on (Lesbian) Gay (and Bisexual) Concerns: 29–30, 37–38,52, 91; Council of Representatives' Resolutions on LGB issues, 9–10, 12, 37, 46, 60; Division 9: Society for the Psychological Study of Social Issues, 29–30, 44, 76; Division 17: Society for Counselling Pyshcology, 9; Division 19: Division for Military Psychology, 60; Division 44: Division for Lesbian and Gay Concerns/ Society for the Psychological Study of Lesbian, Gay Bisexual and Transgender Issues 1, 35–36, 39, 42, 60, 91, 98; Public Policy Office, 28–29; Response to HIV/ AIDS, 28–29, 32–34; Task Forces of the Committee on Lesbian and Gay Concerns, 17, 35; Task Force Report on Gender Identity and Gender Variance (2009), 42, 89–98
American Psychologist, 20, 32–34, 37–39
American Public Health Association
Americans with Disabilities Act, 1990, 37
androcentrism, 10, 37–38, 79–80
anger, 71
Archives of Sexual Behavior, 18, 20, 21, 77
Association for Gay Psychologists, 9
Association for Psychological Science, 40
Association for Women in Psychology, 9
Attitudes *see also* homophobia; functions of, 14, 32–33, 73–74; measurement of, 13–14, 62; polarization following biased assimilation of information, 72–73; sympathetic to homosexuals, 30

Baehr vs Miike (1996), 59
behaviorist psychology, 8, 11, 15, 20, 94–95
Ben-Shalom v Marsh I (1989), 46
biological psychology, 5, 34, 39, 47, 53, 83
bisexuality/bisexual people; recognition in law, 43, 49, 60f; recognition in lesbian and gay psychology, 2, 14, 16, 29, 32–33, 38, 43, 58, 78, 82; *see also* sexual fluidity
Bottoms vs Bottoms (1995), 53
Bowers vs Hardwick, 45–46, 64, 69
Brown vs Board of Education, 44